RAMA and the Early Avatars of Vishnu

RAMA
and the Early Avatars of Vishnu

The Galaxy of Hindu Gods
Book 3

PLUS RAMAYANA ABRIDGED

SWAMI ACHUTHANANDA

Copyright © 2019 Swami Achuthananda

All rights reserved. No part of this book may be reproduced or transmitted in any form or by any means, electronic or mechanical, including photocopying, recording, or by an information storage or retrieval system, without the written permission of the author, except for the inclusion of brief quotations in a review.

The author can be contacted at *swamia@mmmgh.com*

Editor: Polly Kummel, *www.amazinphrasin.com*
Page Layout and Design: *Wordzworth.com*
Cover Design: Cathi Stevenson, *www.BookCoverExpress.com*
Photo Credit: *www.shutterstock.com* and public domain (Wikimedia Commons)

ISBN: 978-0-9757883-4-9

Relianz Communications Pty Ltd,
Queensland 4035, Australia.
Email: *contact@relianz.com.au*

Other books by Swami Achuthananda:

Many Many Many Gods of Hinduism
(A Concise Introduction to Hinduism)

Volumes in **The Galaxy of Hindu Gods** series:
Book One: The Reign of the Vedic Gods
Book Two: The Ascent of Vishnu and the Fall of Brahma
Book Three: Rama and the Early Avatars of Vishnu
Book Four: Krishna and the Later Avatars of Vishnu
Book Five: The Awesome and Fearsome Shiva
Book Six: Devi—Goddesses from Devious Kali to Divine Lakshmi
Book Seven: Bhagavad Gita—An Odyssey of Self-Discovery

*Dedicated to my daughter Rhea,
the avatar of perseverance in my galaxy.*

Contents

Chapter 1	Overview of Dashavataras	1
Chapter 2	Avatar #1 – Matsya or Fish	7
Chapter 3	I'm Born Age after Age	11
Chapter 4	Avatar #2 – Kurma or Turtle	15
Chapter 5	Avatar #3 – Varaha or Boar	21
Chapter 6	Avatar #4 – Narasimha or Man-lion	27
Chapter 7	Avatar #5 – Vamana or Dwarf	35
Chapter 8	Avatar #6 – Parashurama or Rama with an Axe	41
Chapter 9	Amba Loses Her Honor	47
Chapter 10	Kerala – The Land of Parashurama	51
Chapter 11	Avatar #7 Rama – The One Who Provides Light and Joy	55
Chapter 12	The Story of Rama – I	61
Chapter 13	The Story of Rama – II	69
Chapter 14	The Story of Rama – III	75
Chapter 15	Is Rama the Perfect Man?	81
Chapter 16	Ravana – The Greatest Villain of Hinduism	87
Chapter 17	What's in a Name?	95
Chapter 18	Rama Setu – A Man-made Bridge?	99
Chapter 19	The Doggedness of Agni Pariksha	105
Chapter 20	The Ramayana of Valmiki	109
Chapter 21	A Mosque and Temple Controversy	113
Chapter 22	Hanuman – The Ideal Devotee	119

Chapter 23	Hanuman – A Monkey or Ape?	127
Chapter 24	Sankat Mochan Hanuman	131
Chapter 25	The Hundredth Monkey Phenomenon	137
Chapter 26	Dashavataras and Darwin	141
Index		147
What's Coming Up?		155

What good is the warmth of summer,
without the cold of winter to give it sweetness.

—JOHN STEINBECK, 1902–1962

Dear Reader,

The principle of duality says that a phenomenon or thing cannot exist without its opposite. That is, every action has a reaction, every summer has a winter, and every liberal has a conservative. But that's not all. Such paired opposites also include hot-cold, life-death, *deva-asura*, and so on. It's a well-known fact that a positive statement can have an opposite—a negative statement. However, it's a little known fact that a positive statement without a negative statement is usually a platitude. Why? In the absence of a negative narrative, views become one-sided or biased and less credible. Armed with this nugget of insight, we enter the most exciting part of Hindu mythology—the Dashavataras—where we meet the top ten incarnations of Vishnu. You see, until now Vishnu has been sleeping blissfully in that vast ocean of milk. The time has arrived for him to wake up and get involved in the affairs of the world. Through the lens of the duality, we will be examining Vishnu's actions and their ramifications. The enforcement of cosmic law and order spans two volumes—this volume and the next (book 4).

A helicopter view of the avatars is provided early on in this book. Discerning readers will observe a striking similarity between the incarnations of Vishnu and modern evolution theory—and we dedicate a chapter on this topic. As we progress through the avatars, you will notice the concept of dharma (religious duty), which is central to Hinduism, plays a crucial part in human relationships, particularly in the epics Ramayana and Mahabharata. Oh, you haven't read the Ramayana or

Mahabharata? No problem—no karmic points deducted. A shortened version of Ramayana is presented in this book. (Mahabharata is dealt in the fourth volume.) Unlike other books, this book will discuss issues and controversies in detail. The central character of this volume is Rama, the protagonist of the Ramayana and a name that is synonymous with dharma. He is the supreme holder of dharma and the near-perfect deity in Hinduism. If you were to rate all Hindu deities, Rama scores 99.5 percent for perfection. Why not 100 percent? Rama fought with the ten-headed Ravana and vanquished him, but it appears Rama waged a bigger battle with the dictates of dharma—and lost. If *The Reign of the Vedic Gods* (book 1) was about sacrifice and *The Ascent of Vishnu and the Fall of Brahma* (book 2) about bhakti (devotion), this book is about dharma.

In this book we meet the monkey-faced Hanuman for the first time. The quintessential *bhakta* (devotee), Hanuman is associated with Rama and highly revered among the Hindus. We also meet two central characters of Hindu mythology—Prahlada and Ravana. Prahlada came from a family of *asuras* (demons), yet he was able to attain the pinnacle of human life. The story of Prahlada also shows that Vishnu will go to extraordinary lengths to protect his devotees. And while Prahlada was a great devotee of Vishnu, Ravana was Prahlada's antithesis. Hinduism has no villain greater than Ravana. A serial rapist, he was known for abducting women even in ancient times. But not everyone regards Ravana as evil. Some describe him as a devout follower of Shiva, a Vedic scholar, and a fine player of the veena. There are even temples dedicated to Ravana in India and Sri Lanka. In fact many Tamils proudly describe themselves as descendants of Ravana. Hey, what's going on?

This brings us back to the duality principle—that paired opposites are a reality. Duality tells us every phenomenon or aspect of life arises from a balanced interaction of opposite and competing forces. More important, it says that these forces are not just opposites but extremes of the same thing. Heat and cold may appear to be opposites at first glance, but they are simply varying degrees of the same phenomenon. They do not cancel each other; rather, they balance each other like the dual wings of a bird.

There can be no summer without winter. Likewise, there can no Rama without Ravana. It's just that you and I have a tendency to prefer one over the other. Just as Rama is revered for protecting Hindu dharma and restoring world order, Ravana is honored for shielding the island country from foreign invaders and preserving its culture.

There are two sides to a coin but only one coin. Which side will you choose? And whom will you pick—Rama or Ravana?

Swami Achuthananda

Rama clashes with Ravana in the battle of Lanka

1

Overview of Dashavataras

> *To guard the pious, to destroy evil-doers, to establish righteousness, I am born age after age.*
>
> —KRISHNA IN BHAGAVAD GITA 4.8

Avatar means descent and generally refers to the incarnation of a god into an earthly form, such as an animal or a human. It is a hallmark of the Hindu god Vishnu. Hindus believe Vishnu has descended to Earth on many occasions. However, ten such descents are considered more significant than the rest and are collectively known as Dashavataras, or ten descents. But like many things in Hinduism, the list of ten is not fixed. It varies slightly across sects of Hinduism and regions of the country. Three of these avatars were to punish Vishnu's palace guards, who had turned against him. And one did not return after his mission on Earth. Let's take a walk through the Dashavatara forest and briefly meet each avatar face to face.

1. Matsya (fish): A wicked demon pinches the Vedas from Brahma while he is asleep. But Brahma has a habit of sleeping for a long time—4.32

billion years. With the world in grave danger, Vishnu springs into action by taking the form of a giant fish. He not only saves the Vedas but rescues humanity from a great deluge.

2. Kurma (turtle): The demons have become too powerful and take control of the heavens. The gods realize that they must obtain the nectar of immortality to regain power. But the nectar can be obtained only by churning the ocean, a massive task for which they need the help of demons. Using a mountain to roil the waters, the gods and demons embark on this mission, but the mountain starts sinking into the ocean floor. Vishnu comes to their rescue in the form of a giant turtle. After outwitting the demons and obtaining the nectar, the gods regain their power and drive the demons away from heaven.

3. Varaha (boar): A monstrous demon steals Mother Earth and hides her in the bottom of the ocean. Vishnu, assuming the form of a giant boar, dives to the bottom of the ocean, where he battles the demon. After defeating the demon, the boar uses its mighty tusks to heave Earth back above the water. At the end, Mother Earth is not only impressed but becomes romantically involved with her rescuer.

4. Narasimha (man-lion): The demon Hiranyakashipu performs extreme austerities and becomes the ruler of heavens. Once in power, he starts terrorizing the gods. He even harasses his innocent child for being a Vishnu devotee. But Vishnu is known to protect his devotees at any cost. When the child appeals to his lord for help, Vishnu in the form of a man-lion bursts out from one of the giant pillars of the fiend's palace and mauls the demon to death.

5. Vamana (dwarf): A generous but conceited demon, Bali ascends to power and banishes the gods from heaven. The distraught gods petition Vishnu, who takes the form of a dwarf called Vamana. In an effort to take advantage of Bali's generosity, Vamana begs for "three steps" of land. When the wish is granted, Vamana turns into a giant and covers heaven and Earth in two strides. A demon of his word,

Bali offers his own head for the third step and is promptly stomped into the netherworld.

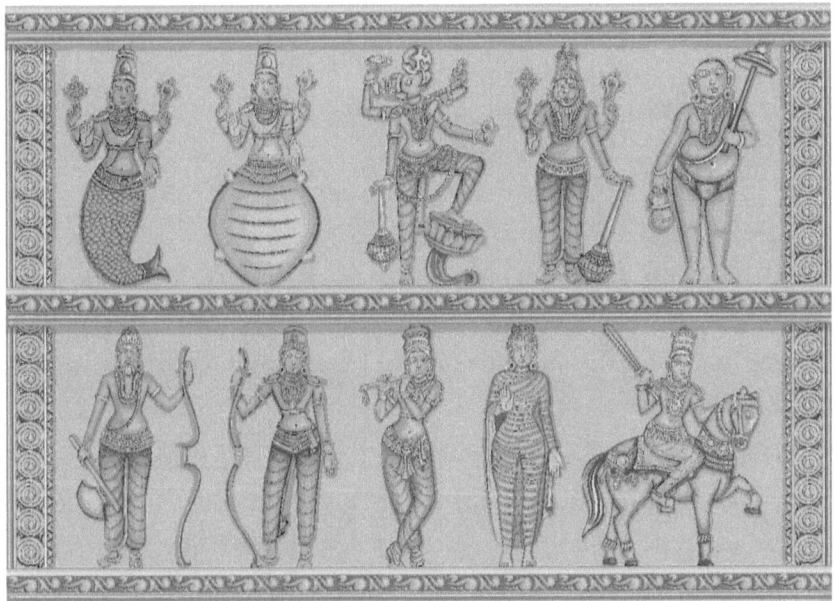

Dashavataras, from top left: Fish, Turtle, Boar, Man-lion, Dwarf, Parashurama, Rama, Krishna, Buddha, and Kalki (image re-created from a stone sculpture)

6 Parashurama (axe-Rama): Unlike the earlier avatars, this incarnation is rooted in caste conflict and is not the consequence of a demon straying from the path of dharma. The warrior caste has become corrupt with power and commit atrocities on peasants from the countryside. When a soldier assaults his father, Parashurama, a Brahmin, slays the soldier with his axe. The army retaliates to avenge the death of the soldier. Parashurama returns the favor by annihilating the entire warrior class and their families.

7 Rama: One of most widely worshipped Hindu deities, Rama is the embodiment of chivalry and virtue. His story is chronicled in the epic Ramayana. Because of a family feud, Rama is exiled to a forest. While at the forest his wife is abducted by the demon king Ravana.

Rama assembles a motley army of monkeys and bears from the forest. He then travels to Lanka and defeats Ravana and his superior forces.

8 Krishna: A prophecy has foretold that the vicious ruler Kamsa will be slain by the eighth child of his sister. The king is deeply troubled and kills every child born to his sister. The eighth child, Krishna, miraculously escapes and grows up in the care of foster parents. Although Kamsa makes numerous attempts on Krishna's life, he is unsuccessful and eventually meets his fate at the hands of Krishna. By this time Krishna has served the purpose of his incarnation, yet he stays on Earth and goes on to play a major noncombat role in the Mahabharata War. No figure in Hinduism is more beloved than Krishna.

9 Buddha-Balarama: The founder of Buddhism, Siddhartha Gautama, is commonly included in the list of Dashavataras in northern India. As an avatar, Buddha is regarded as a compassionate teacher who preached the path of ahimsa (nonviolence). Hindus believe that Vishnu took this avatar to put an end to animal sacrifice, which was widespread at that time. In southern India, however, Balarama (Krishna's older brother) is considered the ninth avatar. Although overshadowed by his illustrious brother, Balarama is celebrated in mythology for his prodigious strength.

10 Kalki: Vishnu's most powerful incarnation is yet to manifest and is reserved for the future. Kalki is prophesied to arrive at the very end of the Kali Yuga, when virtue has completely disappeared from earth. Riding a white horse with a flaming sword in hand, he is believed to usher us into the new era of perfect dharma.

In the Dashavataras Vishnu does not employ a standard approach to solving cosmic problems. As you may have noticed, Vishnu uses a variety of techniques—trickery, cunning, and brute force, among others—to subdue his adversary.

OVERVIEW OF DASHAVATARAS

When did the Dashavataras take place? According to Hinduism, they occurred in various yugas. As we explained earlier in this series, time in Hinduism is represented in cosmic cycles called yugas.[1] The first five avatars happened in the Satya Yuga, the sixth (Parashurama) and seventh (Rama) in the Treta Yuga, and the eighth (Krishna) in the Dvapara Yuga. The Buddha avatar occurred in Kali Yuga, the current age and supposedly the dark ages of Hinduism. Hindus also believe that the Kalki avatar will occur toward the end of Kali Yuga.

Which is the most important of the Dashavataras? Since each incarnation occurred under a unique set of circumstances, no one incarnation is considered superior to the others. However, the best-known and most celebrated avatars are Rama and Krishna. Such is their popularity that most of the other avatars are no longer objects of worship. The devotion to Rama and Krishna has also eclipsed the worship of Vishnu in northern India. Although that could be true in Aryavarta,[2] Vishnu is still an important deity in southern India.

---

[1] The concept of yuga is explained in book 2 of this series.
[2] Aryavarta means "the land of Aryans" and refers to the land between the Himalaya and Vindhya Mountains.

2

Avatar #1 – Matsya or Fish

If a thousand suns were to rise in the heavens at the same time, the blaze of their light would resemble the splendor of that supreme spirit.

—BHAGAVAD GITA 11:12

In pictures Vishnu is often depicted dressed in regal garments and wearing a benign smile. This is a misleading image and nothing like his true form. The cosmic form of Vishnu—officially known as Vishvarupa—is a stupendous sight that frightens people and makes them dizzy. Only a handful of people have seen this cosmic form in Hindu mythology. One person horrified by Vishnu's colossal form was the ancient king Manu. Unlike others, Manu did not actually see the Vishvarupa. The ever-increasing size of a small fish, however, made him suspect that this was something beyond human contemplation. We now describe the details of Manu's encounter with Vishnu as Matsya (fish), the first of the Dashavataras.

The son of the sun god Surya, Manu was an able ruler, always concerned about the welfare of his subjects. The *pralaya*[3] was fast approaching,

---

[3] The dissolution of the world is called *pralaya* and is described in detail in book 2 of this series.

so Manu became worried about his subjects and the future of humanity. One day he handed his kingdom over to his son and headed to the forest to practice asceticism. After a thousand years Brahma was pleased by Manu's austerities and granted him a boon. Manu asked that he be chosen as the protector of all living beings when the dissolution takes place. Brahma granted this wish and then went to sleep. As soon as Brahma dozed off, the Vedas dribbled from his mouth into the ocean. About this time, a mischievous demon by the name of Hayagriva seized this opportunity to grab the Vedas and ran off with them. No one in the heavens noticed this except Vishnu.

Image re-created from a stone engraving of the Matsya avatar

Back at his hermitage, Manu was performing his daily oblation in a river when a little fish leaped into his hands along with the water. As he was about to put the fish back into the water, it cried out, "Please help me. Save me from the bigger fish!" Sympathetic to its plight, Manu took the fish to his hermitage and put it in an earthen pot. Within a day and half the fish outgrew the pot. Manu transferred the fish to a well, but within no time the fish could not fit into the well. Manu then threw the fish into the river Ganges. The fish continued to grow, so Manu moved it to the ocean. When the fish pervaded the whole ocean, Manu realized this was no ordinary fish. Frightened, he prostrated before the fish and cried, "Who are you, lord? Why are doing this to me?"

The fish thanked Manu for his kindness and revealed its identity as an avatar of Vishnu. The fish then warned Manu that the entire planet would be destroyed in a flood in the coming days. It advised Manu to build a boat to save himself, the seven *rishis* (sages), and the essence of all living creatures on Earth. Just as the fish foretold, clouds began to cover the sky, and torrential rains fell on Earth. As the waters rose dangerously high, Manu took shelter in the ship. But the ship merely drifted in the ocean without a purpose. Suddenly the fish swam up to the ship with a horn on its head. It asked Manu to fasten the ship to its horn. The fish then towed the ship with its horn. When they reached the high ground of the northern mountains (the Himalayas), the fish instructed Manu to tether the ship to a tree. "When the water recedes, get off the ship and descend the mountain," said the fish and bade good-bye to Manu. It then concentrated on another task—saving the Vedas. After the initial wave of the flood had subsided, Vishnu confronted Hayagriva. The demon fought with all his might, but he was no match for Vishnu, who retrieved the Vedas from him.

Meanwhile, Manu, as instructed, carefully made his descent after the floods had receded. He became the sole survivor on Earth, as the rest of the creatures had been washed away by the floods. Manu then embarked on the task of repopulating the world. Oblivious to the dramatic events of the night, Brahma woke up from his long sleep of 4.32 billion years and was greeted by a beaming Vishnu with the Vedas in his hands.

If you have previously heard a different version of this myth, please be reminded that the Matsya avatar has many versions.[4] The tale is described in the Mahabharata, the Shatapatha Brahmana, Bhagavata Purana, Matsya Purana, and others, and no two are alike. In the Mahabharata the fish is actually described as an avatar of Brahma, but the Puranas assert that it was indeed Vishnu. As for the Manu who survived the flood, he is known by many names: Satyavrata, Sraddhadeva, and the popular Vaivasvata Manu.

Among the avatars of Vishnu, Matsya is not as popular as Rama or Krishna. For that reason only a few temples are dedicated to Matsya—these include the Shankhodara temple at Bet Dwarka, Gujarat, and the Vedanarayana Swami temple in Nagalapuram, Andhra Pradesh. Despite its lack of popularity, the Matsya avatar holds great significance in the

---

[4] Another version of this myth appears in book 2 of this series.

Vaishnava tradition. It represents the notion that life originated in water—something we will explore later in this book.

> *Nothing is softer or more flexible than water,*
> *yet nothing can resist it.*
>
> —LAO TZU

3

I'm Born Age after Age

Let's pause and ponder. So what, exactly, is an avatar? *Avatar* can mean different things to different people. For some it may remind them of the 2009 James Cameron's movie *Avatar*. For video game aficionados, avatar is the online representation of your physical presence. That means you could be Nathan in person, but on a computer screen you are represented by your avatar—a silkworm—as in Nathan's case. Guess what? The original meaning of the word was in fact just the opposite. In Sanskrit, the language of origin, *avatar* means descent, or, more precisely, "god crossing over." It is the arrival of an abstract deity in a certain physical form.[5] In Hindu mythology *avatar* means the incarnation of a god in earthly form, such as an animal or a human. Thus the avatar is in essence the transformation of the abstract to the physical—not the other way around—even though the original idea has been turned on its head by computer games. *Avatar* is most often associated with Vishnu and refers to his various forms of incarnation, such as Rama and Krishna.

---

[5] Avatar can be looked upon as the Saguna Brahman, the embodiment of the formless, abstract Nirguna Brahman. We discuss Brahman and these two aspects of Brahman in book 2 of this series.

avatar noun
av·a·tar | \ ˈa-və-ˌtär 🔊 \

Definition of *avatar*
1 : the incarnation of a Hindu deity (such as Vishnu)

And what, exactly, is incarnation? In case you haven't been paying attention, the almighty has been making his appearance in physical forms to convey a powerful message or accomplish a task. *Incarnation* carries the notion of a physical birth and then undergoing the life experience of human beings. Yet incarnations are not the only way a god registers his physical presence. A god can also do so through manifestations—without undergoing a physical birth or life experience. The destroyer god Shiva, for instance, manifests as a tribal warrior in the Mahabharata and challenges the protagonist, Arjuna, to a duel to test his devotion and determination. While manifestations are Shiva's preferred modus operandi, Vishnu has a penchant for avatars. This highlights one key difference between Shiva and Vishnu, the two supergods of Hinduism who have a combined following of more than one billion worshippers.[6]

Strictly speaking, an incarnation is an intervention in the affairs of the world. Given a choice, both Vishnu and Shiva prefer to mind their own business most of the time—Vishnu in blissful slumber and Shiva in profound meditation. Then why do these supergods abandon their comfort zones and come to our not-so-perfect world? The reason is that, while the law of karma acts independently to create a fair, self-governing system of justice, sometimes karmic comeuppance alone may not deter someone from causing a cosmic imbalance through their actions. It is then that a god decides to become involved in the affairs of the world.

As the protector of the universe, Vishnu on many occasions assumed various physical forms to destroy evil and establish the reign of righteousness. Says Krishna in the Bhagavad Gita:

---
[6] Shiva is described in detail in book 5 of this series.

I'M BORN AGE AFTER AGE

Yada yada hi dharmasya glanir bhavati bharata
Abhyuthanam adharmasya tadatmanam srijamy aham
Paritranaya sadhunam vinashaya cha dushkritam
Dharma-samsthapanarthaya sambhavami yuge yuge

(Whenever righteousness wanes, O descendant of Bharata,
And unrighteousness ascends, I bring myself to bodied birth
To guard the pious, to destroy evil-doers,
To establish righteousness, I am born age after age)

"*Sambhavami yuge yuge,*" says Krishna (Vishnu), that is, "I am born age after age." For that reason, there has been no shortage of avatars. Thirty-nine avatars are recorded in accounts of Pancharatra, an ancient Vaishnava[7] tradition. The list of avatars includes Garuda, Vishnu's steed, and the serpent Ananda Shesha. Sometimes local deities like Jagannath and Venkateswara are also considered avatars. According to scholars, the doctrine of avatars allowed important local deities to be incorporated in the pantheon as forms of Vishnu.

Even though the scriptures mention many avatars, ten are considered most important. These are the Dashavataras: Matsya (fish), Kurma (tortoise), Varaha (boar), Narasimha (man-lion), Vamana (dwarf), Parashurama, Rama, Krishna, Buddha, and Kalki. Of these avatars, the first four are nonhuman, while the rest are human forms. The last, Kalki, is yet to arrive and is supposed to bring an end to this world. Balarama, the brother of Krishna, is sometimes considered an avatar replacing Buddha.

The Dashavataras are sometimes viewed as representing the evolution of life and society on Earth. In this depiction, Matsya represents life in water; Kurma, the stage of amphibians; Varaha, life on land; Narasimha, the stage of mammals; Vamana, the development of humans; Parashurama, the development of society; Rama, the formation of nations; Krishna, the advancement in culture and civilization; and Buddha, social advancement.

---

[7] Vaishnavas are Vishnu worshippers.

Hindus consider the seventh and eighth incarnations of Vishnu—Rama and Krishna—the most significant. Rama is often associated with dharma, the caste-based obligations of Hindus. (We will examine this in detail later in this book.) The arrival of Krishna introduced the concept of bhakti (devotion). Since Brahmanic times Hindus have believed that the ultimate aspiration of humans should not be a progressive rise through many lives (and castes) to reach Indra's heaven. Rather, the ultimate aim should be to achieve *moksha* (liberation) through extreme asceticism and yogic meditation. In the course of the epic Mahabharata, Krishna introduces the notion that devotion can also lead to *moksha*—which many devotees found more fulfilling than asceticism or meditation.

Earlier we described the first avatar. We will continue our discussion on Dashavataras in the next several chapters. You will be surprised to know that the concept of *avatar* is not found in the Vedas, the sacred book of the Hindus. The Rigveda, however, describes the celebrated "three steps" of Vishnu as Trivikrama, by which he strode over the universe—and subsequently morphed into the Vamana (dwarf) avatar. Many Puranas (ancient texts), including Agni Purana, Garuda Purana, Bhagavata Purana, and others, describe the Dashavataras. Not all descriptions are identical; for instance, some are described as avatars of Brahma, not Vishnu. There are also contradictions in timeline, as we will point out. All these variations have resulted in the existence of many versions of these incarnations.

> *Inside each of us, there is the seed of both good and evil.*
> *It's a constant struggle as to which one will win.*
> *And one cannot exist without the other.*
>
> —ERIC BURDON, 1941–

❋ ❋ ❋

4

Avatar #2 – Kurma or Turtle

Negligence is the rust of the soul that corrodes through all her best resolves.

—OWEN FELTHAM (1602–1668)

If a simple act of kindness led to the first avatar, negligence was the catalyst for the second. The sage Durvasa once happened to meet Indra, who was riding on the back of an elephant. As a mark of respect, Durvasa removed the garland he was wearing and offered it to Indra, the ruler of the heavens. Indra proudly accepted the garland but carelessly placed it around the trunk of the elephant. The animal threw the garland to the ground and stomped on it. If any other sage had been in this situation, life would have moved forward normally. A spiritual scientist—whom Hindus call *rishi*—Durvasa had conquered the frontiers of the mind and holds a lofty place among his disciples. Yet he had difficulty controlling his own temper. Extremely sensitive to insults, Durvasa became livid at seeing his garland smashed on the ground. He put a curse on the gods that they would soon lose their divine powers.

Durvasa's words came true. Shortly thereafter Indra and the gods lost their battle against the demons, and the demons took control of heaven. Bereft of wealth and power, the gods went to Vishnu for help. He advised them that the only way to regain power was to drink *amrita*, the nectar of immortality. But *amrita* can be obtained only by churning the large ocean. The gods realized they were not strong enough for this task, for

The churning of the milky ocean, 19th-century painting by Raja Ravi Varma

AVATAR #2–KURMA OR TURTLE

Durvasa's curse had sapped their strength. They decided to enlist the demons by promising to share *amrita* with them

Soon the churning of the ocean began in earnest. First potent herbs were thrown on the waters. Next, the gods and demons uprooted Mount Mandara, a spur of Mount Meru, and used it as a churning staff. The serpent Vasuki, often found coiled around Shiva's neck, wrapped itself around the staff and became the churning rope. As the churning began, the demons insisted on holding the head of the snake, while the gods, taking advice from Vishnu, agreed to hold its tail. The poisonous fumes of the serpent, however, exhausted the strength of the demons. Despite this, the gods and demons alternately pulled back and forth on the snake's body, causing the mountain to rotate, which in turn churned the ocean.

As the churning continued with great vigor, the mountain began to sink to the bottom of the ocean, much to the dismay of the deities. Vishnu came to the rescue in the form of a giant turtle called Kurma and supported the mountain on its curved back. The gods and demons were relieved, and churning resumed. The first thing to emerge from the ocean—to everyone's disbelief—was the most virulent poison, Halahala, which horrified the deities and threatened the existence of every living being in the world. As Halahala started spreading into the ocean, Shiva gathered all the poison with his hands and swallowed it in one gulp, leaving his bystanders stunned. Parvati rushed to her husband's aid and pressed his neck with her hands, ensuring the poison remained stuck forever in his throat. The poison, however, turned Shiva's throat blue. That is why Shiva is often called Neelakanta, the one with blue throat.

With the poison removed from the waters, the ocean was rendered safe. The gods and demons pressed on with the task of churning the ocean. A number of precious objects, once thought lost in the *pralaya*, rose up out of the ocean. They included Kaustubha (the jewel worn by Vishnu), the Parijata tree (the celestial wish-giving tree), and Sharanga (a powerful bow). Several deities also rose to the surface. They included Chandra (the moon that adorned Shiva's head), Lakshmi (the goddess of wealth, who accepted Vishnu as her eternal consort), Rambha (a nymph who became the first of the *apsaras*), Varuni (the goddess of wine), Uchchaihsravas (the beautiful white horse given to the demon Bali but later seized by Indra), and Airavata (the elephant that became Indra's mount after he stopped riding the horse). Finally the grand moment arrived with the appearance of Dhanavantari, the lord of physicians, holding a bowl of *amrita*, the much sought-after nectar of immortality.

In the midst of these developments, the demons had made a secret plan. As soon as Dhanavantari emerged from the ocean, the demons snatched the pot of nectar from him and made a run for it. Thus the demons voided the original agreement of sharing the nectar equally among the gods and demons. A squabble soon broke out among the *asuras* themselves as to who should be served first. Meanwhile, the indignant gods appealed to Vishnu, who decided it was time for his second act, this time as the femme fatale Mohini.

With a face like a flowering lotus, Mohini appeared among the demons; she was clad in a sari, her ankle bracelets jingling as she strode toward them. The demons were thunderstruck at her beauty, their mouths wide open like African hippos in combat. The beauty of Mohini was so enthralling that the demons forgot about the ambrosia in their custody. As Mohini looked askance at the bowl of ambrosia, a wise *asura* suggested perhaps she should decide how the demons should share the divine nectar. All the demons cheered at this suggestion.

Mohini decided that both the gods and the demons had toiled hard to get the *amrita*. Therefore they were entitled to an equal share. Understandably the demons were not keen on this idea, but they decided not to object to it. Mohini then asked the gods and demons to sit in two rows. She took the nectar and served the row of gods first. After the last god had been served, she vanished with the bowl. With Mohini missing in action, the demons figured the divine damsel had snookered them. But she had not outwitted all the demons. Knowing this was a ploy, the *asura* Rahuketu took the form of a god and drank the *amrita*. However, the sun and moon gods, who were sitting next to the demon, recognized the charlatan and promptly informed Vishnu. Before Rahuketu could ingest the nectar, Vishnu took his divine discus, Sudarshana Chakra, and hurled it at the demon, splitting his body in two. Because the nectar had entered his throat, Rahuketu survived and later became two planets. His head became the planet Rahu and his torso Ketu. Rahu and Ketu became perennial enemies of the sun and moon. According to legend, eclipses are caused when these demons try to devour their arch enemies.

When the demons realized they had been hoodwinked, they became furious and charged at the gods. But the gods, fortified by the *amrita*, were easily able to repel the demons, who had been weakened by Vasuki's breath. Thus the gods became victors in the quest for the elixir of immortality and the undisputed rulers of the universe. Immortality also gave *devas* (demi-gods) a strategic advantage in their perennial fights against the demons.

The churning of the ocean, which Hindus call *samudra manthan*, is a crucial event in Hindu mythology. As Kurma, and then as the gorgeous sari-clad Mohini, Vishnu plays a double role in this avatar.[8] Discerning readers will be baffled by the appearance of the elephant Airavata among the many treasures discovered in the ocean. You may recall that the whole churning operation owed to the elephant's tantrum in the first place, yet the pachyderm seems to have been found during the massive undertaking by gods and demons. The same can be said about the horse Uchchaihsravas. According to mythology, Uchchaihsravas was given to the demon king Bali but seized by Indra, who made it his mount. Later in life Indra abandoned the horse and used the elephant Airavata as his ride. But Bali makes his notable appearance only in the Vamana avatar (avatar #5) of the Dashavataras.

The truth is that myths are teeming with inconsistencies as stories are told and retold. Hinduism explains away this inconsistency through the notion of *manvantaras*,[9] which are cycles of creation and dissolution

---

[8] Vishnu also plays a double role in both the Rama and Krishna avatars.
[9] The concept of manvantara is explained in book 2 of this series.

in the life of Brahma. According to this belief, Indra is only an administrative position and Airavata was his elephant in an earlier *manvantara*. The elephant was trapped in the sea at the *pralaya*, only to be recovered during the churning of the milky ocean.

Like other myths, the Kurma avatar has many variations.[10] Although Vishnu's role in the Kurma avatar was limited compared to that in other avatars, Kurma is still acknowledged as an important figure in Hindu cosmology. While many temple walls, including one in the famous Angkor Wat, depict the churning of the milky ocean, only a few temples are dedicated to Kurma; most are in the Indian state of Andhra Pradesh.

More popular than Kurma is Vishnu's Mohini avatar. The popularity of Mohini stems from her role as the mother of Ayyappan, the deity of Sabarimala, a famous sacred site in South India. Open for only two months of the year, the Sabarimala shrine, located among eighteen hills, attracts about 20 million devotees yearly.

---

[10] Another version of this myth appears in book 2 of this series.

5

Avatar #3 – Varaha or Boar

> *The trees are our lungs, the rivers our circulation, the air our breath, and the earth our body.*
>
> —DEEPAK CHOPRA, 1946–

Somewhere along the way a sage is offended by a reckless act and feels disrespected. He unleashes a punishing curse that can be circumvented only by the intervention of the supreme gods. Sound familiar? This was the backdrop of the Kurma avatar. The next avatar in the Dashavatara series—the boar, or Varaha—is no different. The genesis of this avatar goes back to an incident at Vaikuntha, the celestial abode of Vishnu. The Kumaras, a quartet of sages who dress half-naked and roam around as children, are paying a visit to Vishnu when they are stopped at the gate and interrogated by the gatekeepers, Jaya and Vijaya. Because the Kumaras are quite short, the guards mistake them for naughty kids and use large clubs to shoo them away. Humiliated, the Kumaras put a terrible curse on Jaya and Vijaya, condemning them to spend several lifetimes on Earth as demons and engage in hateful acts against their beloved lord, Vishnu.

Devastated, the guards were further stunned to learn that curses can rarely be withdrawn. They soon felt the effect of the curse. Their memories wiped clean, Jaya and Vijaya were transported to Earth, where they were reborn as Hiranyakashipu and Hiranyaksha to the illustrious duo of Diti and Kashyapa. The planet shook violently at their birth. There were hurricanes, fires, lightning, and thunder all over the world. The giant waves of the ocean wailed loudly. "If there is so much chaos at birth itself, what will happen when they grow up?" Indra wondered. Despite the inauspicious signs at their birth, the Hiranya brothers grew up into strong and fearless kids and became known as the golden boys.[11] As they reached adulthood, their courage and strength also grew. The younger one, Hiranyaksha, whose name means golden-eyed, was extremely ambitious.[12] He undertook austerities for a thousand years and impressed Brahma, who believed that anyone who performed such extreme austerities deserved to be rewarded regardless of their motives. So Brahma granted Hiranyaksha the boon of invulnerability. This was when things started to change for the demon, as his evil tendencies soon began to surface.

Emboldened by the boon, Hiranyaksha began committing atrocities against both mortals and gods. Unlike other demons before him, he assaulted the defenseless Mother Earth, Bhudevi, who was floating on the ocean, and shoved her deep into the primordial waters. The demigod Varuna, the guardian of the waters, attempted to stop the demon, but he was no match for the demon's incredible strength. By now Brahma was having second thoughts about granting the boon to the demon. The distressed gods, led by Brahma, appealed to Vishnu for divine assistance.

---

[11] Hiranya means gold in Sanskrit.

[12] There is some confusion about which twin is older, Jaya or Vijaya. Among the gatekeepers, Jaya is generally considered older. Likewise Hiranyakashipu, having come out of the womb first, is considered the older brother of Hiranyaksha, although many texts state the opposite.

AVATAR #3 – VARAHA OR BOAR

Then a strange thing happened. A tiny beast emerged from one of Brahma's nostrils. The beast took the form of a boar and then grew rapidly—like the little fish in the Matsya avatar. Soon its size increased to that of an elephant and then to that of a colossal mountain. As the boar roared, the sages recognized Vishnu in his Varaha avatar and began chanting hymns in praise of the god. Mighty as a lion, Varaha had sharp white tusks with eyes that flashed like lightning. The animal plunged

Image of the Varaha avatar taken from a stone engraving

Sculpture of Varaha inside Rani Ki Vav, a UNESCO World Heritage Site, Gujarat, India

into the depths of the water where it encountered Hiranyaksha, who stopped Varaha and challenged the beast to a duel. Varaha ignored the demon's threat and raised Bhudevi with its tusks, rescuing her from the

AVATAR #3—VARAHA OR BOAR

demon's clutches. The furious demon charged toward the boar with a mace. The two fought fiercely with maces for a thousand years. Years of fighting sapped the strength of the demon. Eventually Varaha pierced the demon's heart with one of its tusks. The animal then rose from the ocean with Mother Earth cradled in its tusks and placed her gently on the ocean. She floated like a ship, and her massive expanse prevented her from sinking. With the demon vanquished, the gods and sages rejoiced, falling at Varaha's feet.

Meanwhile, Bhudevi, no longer a captive in the sea, fell in love with her rescuer. Ancient texts state the boar was so virile that it even begot a child from this union, for a great mass emerged from her belly and soared to the sky. Hindus believe her son became the planet Mars.

Stripped of its mythical trappings, the Varaha avatar evokes a major geological event. In fact many scholars have noted that the story of the boar avatar has an uncanny resemblance to an asteroid that struck Earth, perhaps after sea levels began to rise at the end of the Ice Age. For Hindus the coming of Varaha symbolizes the resurrection of Earth after a *pralaya* and the start of a new age. Many temples are dedicated to Varaha and are located across India in many states. The most prominent ones include the Sri Varahaswami Temple in Tirumala, Andhra Pradesh, and the Bhuvarahaswami Temple near Chidambaram, Tamil Nadu.

Curious readers must be wondering why Hiranyaksha died even after obtaining the boon of invulnerability from attacks. The fact is boons are designed by clever divine minds and come with loopholes, fine print, escape clauses, and use-by dates. They are often called "boons of conditional immortality." In this case, when Hiranyaksha was asking Brahma for the boon, he listed the names of all gods, men, and animals from whom he wished to be immune, but he forgot to mention the boar. Vishnu seized on this omission to end Hiranyaksha's reign of terror. Upon completion of his mission, Hiranyaksha did not resume guard duties at Vaikuntha; rather, he began preparations for his next mission on Earth. The Kumaras may have been physically short, but their curses were extra long. The original curse stipulated that the gatekeepers had to serve seven lifetimes on Earth. After the frightened guards begged for forgiveness, their punishment was commuted to three lifetimes.[13]

So what happened to Hiranyaksha's brother? Hiranyakashipu is still serving his first sentence on Earth, but he was outraged to learn of his brother's demise. "The Supreme Lord is supposed to treat the gods and demons equally. Because the gods pleaded for help from Vishnu, he killed my dear brother." Simmering with anger, he set his mind to destroying Vishnu and his followers—which we will discuss in the next chapter.

> *When you do something noble and beautiful and nobody noticed, do not be sad. For the sun every morning is a beautiful spectacle and yet most of the audience still sleeps.*
>
> —JOHN LENNON, 1940-1980

---

[13] As *asuras*, Jaya and Vijaya served as Hiranyakashipu and Hiranyaksha in their first lifetime, Ravana and Kumbhakarna in their second lifetime, and Shishupala and the relatively unknown Dantavakra in their third lifetime.

6

Avatar #4 – Narasimha or Man-lion

Prayer is the key of the morning and the bolt of the evening.

—MAHATMA GANDHI, 1869–1948

According to Hindu beliefs, Vishnu resides in the highest realm of the universe in his celestial city called Vaikuntha (also known as the place of no hindrance), where he sits on a throne, flanked by his wife and the giant snake Shesha. The city has streets covered in gold and buildings lined with jewels; it is located in the direction of the constellation Capricorn. If Vaikuntha is located in another realm and light-years from our planet, how can Vishnu hear the call of his devotees when they seek his help? Back in the 1970s, the noted South Indian poet Sreekumaran Thampi answered this query when he wrote, "God exists in earth, heaven, pillars, and rust. Compassionate, he lives as the vigil of our hearts." [14]

---

[14] The lyrics are translated from the Malayalam devotional song, Mannilum Vinnilum, composed for the movie Swami Ayyappan (1975).

According to Thampi, Vishnu may be residing in Vaikuntha, but he is omnipresent and pervades the entire universe. The popular lines of Thampi's also capture the essence of Narasimha, or the Man-lion avatar of Vishnu. Like other avatars of Vishnu, the man-lion avatar arrives to restore the cosmic balance thrown out of equilibrium by the disproportionate power of an individual. This avatar, however, is particularly significant since it reinforces some of the key ideas of Hinduism that are seldom highlighted in the scriptures, although they always are observed in spirit.

As the gatekeeper of Vishnu, Jaya was the epitome of dharma. For Jaya no lord was greater than Vishnu. Because the Kumaras put a curse on him, Jaya's subtle body was transported to Earth, where he was reborn to a famous demon clan. Legend has it that when the sage Kashyapa was performing an extravagant sacrifice, his wife, Diti, gave birth to the first twin, who immediately walked into the sacrifice room, sat on the golden seat, and chanted sacred texts, to the bewilderment of the priests. The parents called the child Hiranyakashipu, which means "the golden clad." Within minutes the second twin, Hiranyaksha, was also born.

Both Hiranyaksha and Hiranyakashipu grew up to be commanding warriors. Powerfully built and confident of their strength, the brothers challenged the gods to a duel, but the gods, sensing they were no match, panicked and disappeared. Hiranyakashipu was a staunch devotee of Vishnu's in his earlier life, but in his new life he became the opposite, a sworn enemy of Vishnu's. When Hiranyakashipu learned that Vishnu had slain his twin brother, the demon was outraged. Seething, he hurried to Vishnu's residence with a trident. But the pervasive Vishnu saw him coming and assumed an invisible form. The demon bellowed loudly and, upon finding no one, searched for Vishnu everywhere: forests, caves, oceans, and even planets. But he could not find him anywhere.

Frustrated, Hiranyakashipu soon realized the futility of his search. Vishnu was no ordinary god. He was extremely powerful, and to defeat him the demon would have to become equal to Vishnu or even more powerful than he was. The only recourse was to embark on a rigorous

AVATAR #4—NARASIMHA OR MAN-LION

regimen of austerity. The demon headed to Mount Mandara and stood upright with his arms upraised and his gaze focused on the sky. It was an exceedingly difficult pose to maintain, but extreme ambition made him hold the posture for years.

From the heavens, Indra, the ruler of the heavens, learned about Hiranyakashipu's extreme *tapas* (asceticism). This was the opportunity for the gods to regroup, for they had been driven away from their abodes by the Hiranya twins. Indra and other *devas* noticed that Hiranyakashipu's palace was unguarded and went there and arrested his pregnant queen. As Indra was leading her away, the sage Narada mystically appeared before them and ordered Indra to release the queen. "She is sinless and chaste, not to mention another man's wife," Narada warned.

"But that Hiranyakashipu's baby is growing in this woman," Indra protested. "If she gives birth to a boy, he'll be as unhinged as his father."

Narada assured Indra that this was not going to happen. "I will take custody of the mother, and the boy will be protected by Vishnu." Turning to the queen, Narada promised her safe passage and complete protection. He took her to his hermitage in the forest and told her to remain there until her husband completed his austerities and returned to the palace.

At the hermitage the queen felt at home in the company of the sage and honored him with utmost reverence. Narada taught her about karma and transcendental knowledge. Unknown to them, the boy within her womb listened intently to the sage's wisdom—lessons that would shape his future and alter the demonic dynasty.

Meanwhile Hiranyakashipu's years of austerity did not go unnoticed in the heavens. Brahma was impressed and granted him a boon. "Please grant me immortality, dear lord!" Hiranyakashipu pleaded. Brahma balked. He himself was mortal, and of the gods forming the Trimurti, he had the shortest life span. "Ask me for anything other than immortality," Brahma replied. Since immortality was off the table, the next best thing would be something close to it: near-immortality, which means death can happen only in highly unlikely circumstances. "O lord, let me not be killed by man or beast or god, by day or night, and neither indoors nor outdoors," Hiranyakashipu besought. The blessings Hiranyakashipu had requested were unobtainable by most living beings, but Brahma granted them to the demon nevertheless. The demon had achieved a perfection in his austerities.

Empowered by the boon, Hiranyakashipu, like his brother, wasted little time driving away the gods and becoming the ruler of the universe. He appropriated Indra's palace with all its opulence and made it his new headquarters. Hiranyakashipu was not finished. He wanted to be the focal point. Hence he summarily banned worship of other gods. This forced everyone to worship him as the supreme lord instead of Vishnu. Sacrifices henceforth were to be performed exclusively to him—not to other gods. Hiranyakashipu's cunning plan was to starve the gods of offerings by banning sacrifices to them. Without offerings, the gods would perish. Hiranyakashipu would then become the one and only god—which would be the sweetest revenge against Vishnu.

At his palace one day Hiranyakashipu summoned his teachers to bring his five-year-old son, Prahlada, to his chamber. When the child arrived, the demon affectionately put him on his lap and asked, "Son, you have been learning lessons from your teachers. What is the greatest lesson you received from them so far?" Earnestly, the child replied, "My spiritual master Narada taught me that anyone who has accepted a temporary body and a temporary household life is full of worries. One should therefore abandon that life, retreat to the forest, and take shelter in Vishnu." The demon could not believe what he was hearing. His own son was asking him to take refuge in Vishnu, his sworn enemy. But Prahlada was only a child, so Hiranyakashipu reprimanded his teachers. He cautioned them to safeguard Prahlada from the influence of Vishnu devotees.

At another time Hiranyakashipu invited Prahlada to his quarters and asked him, "Little one, you have been learning many things from your teachers. What's the most valuable lesson you have learned from them?" Without a moment's hesitation Prahlada reeled off in his childish innocence: "I believe chanting the glories of Vishnu, surrendering completely to him, and serving him lifelong is the best of that knowledge.

AVATAR #4 – NARASIMHA OR MAN-LION

Whoever dedicates his life to serving Vishnu is the most learned person." The demon was dumbfounded. Was he hearing this right? His own son once again was extolling his father's enemy even after the child had been warned not to do so.

The demon could no longer control his rage. "You defiant fool," he screamed. Summoning his guards, he ordered them to flog the child. The guards struck Prahlada's tender body repeatedly, but the boy sat silently without protest. When Hiranyakashipu realized that the punishment was not working, he had the boy lowered into a pit of poisonous snakes. But soon he noticed that the fangs of the snakes were broken and their crests had burst, whereas Prahlada remained unscathed. Furious, Hiranyakashipu had him thrown beneath the feet of elephants. But elephants as vast as mountains could not hurt Prahlada. Hiranyakashipu then had Prahlada hurled from the top of a mountain—all to no avail. No matter what Hiranyakashipu did, a mystical power seemed to protect the boy.

Exasperated, Hiranyakashipu ordered his son to be brought to his chamber at once. The boy stood before the demon looking serene and peaceful. "You stubborn rascal. You are an unworthy son, not fit to live in this world. You have no idea about my powers. Do you know that when I am angry, the earth shakes and the planets tremble? By whose power have you become so bold and powerful?" Hiranyakashipu barked. The boy replied, "Father, the source of my power is the same as yours—the supreme god, Vishnu!" The very mention of the name Vishnu seemed to touch a particularly sensitive nerve in the demon.

"You ungrateful scoundrel! If Vishnu is the greatest, then go ask him to save your life. Where is he? Why can't I find him anywhere?" Pointing to the ground, Hiranyakashipu growled, "Is he present on earth?" Seeing Prahlada nod, Hiranyakashipu pointed upward and said, "What about the heaven?" to which Prahlada replied nonchalantly, "He is present everywhere, Father." Hiranyakashipu couldn't stand his son's unflinching devotion to Vishnu anymore. "Everywhere, really? Is he then present in this pillar?" Without waiting for an answer, the demon, in a fit of rage, took his mace and swung at the pillar, smashing it into pieces.

The sound of the pillar shattering reverberated throughout palace. Courtiers rushed to the king's chamber to see what had happened. As the noise subsided, it was followed by a moment of deafening silence. Then, from inside the column, came a terrifying sound that was even louder. An incredible creature emerged from the debris, roaring and raging. It had the face of a lion and the body of a man—a man-lion. Everybody in the palace was frightened at this monstrous creature. Hiranyakashipu looked at it with disbelief. From above the gods celebrated, savoring the moment. Vishnu had finally arrived in his avatar as Narasimha. The demon's reign of terror was going to end.

As the creature moved toward him, Hiranyakashipu grabbed his mace. Lunging forward, he swung wildly at the man-lion. He missed and landed in front of the beast, who caught him swiftly. Screaming and squirming, Hiranyakashipu somehow managed to wriggle away. Freed from the creature's hold, he dashed to his chambers to grab his sword.

Sword in hand, Hiranyakashipu became more assured. When he turned, he winced in fear, for he could see the man-lion was waiting for him in the palace doorway. Mustering cour-

Image of the Narasimha avatar taken from a stone engraving

age, Hiranyakashipu headed toward Narasimha to confront the beast. As Hiranyakashipu got closer, he became more desperate and waved his sword in every direction, hoping one would connect with the creature. The man-lion was quicker than what Hiranyakashipu anticipated. The creature seized Hiranyakashipu with enormous strength and placed him on his lap as effortlessly as placing a baby. With his sharp claws Narasimha tore the demon's entrails from his abdomen, killing him instantly.

AVATAR #4 – NARASIMHA OR MAN-LION

Wall art of Narasimha mauling the demon Hiranyakashipu at a Hindu temple in Mayapur, West Bengal, India

The sudden and violent death of the demon shocked the people in the palace. In the heavens the gods rejoiced at the victory of Vishnu over the ruthless demon. Vishnu was able to orchestrate Hiranyakashipu's death outside the conditions of Brahma's boon, for the time was evening (neither day nor night), the place was the doorway of the palace (not inside or outside), and the assailant was a man-lion (not human, beast, or god). It is said that after killing Hiranyakashipu, none of the demigods was able to calm Narasimha's fury. Then, at the request of Brahma, Prahlada approached Vishnu and was able to pacify him. Later Vishnu installed the righteous Prahlada as the king of the realm.

Although the Narasimha avatar has an element of brutality, it highlights several facets of Hinduism. First, Vishnu will protect his devotees no matter how extraordinary the circumstances may be. Second, the Supreme Being permeates everywhere: in the sky, Earth, pillars, the smallest twig, and even in rust. Third, and most important, the god does not care whether you are born as a *deva* or an *asura*, for your actions determine your karma. Prahlada was a demon's son, but he was not intrinsically evil. Like the sun and moon and stars, who have their rightful places in the universe, all kinds of beings have their places in the Hindu cosmos.

More than a dozen versions of the Narasimha avatar appear in the Puranas. It is one of the popular avatars of Vishnu and next only to the Rama and Krishna avatars. In the Narasimha avatar valor is celebrated as an aspect of divinity. While the human is the most powerful of all creatures, the lion is the most valiant among lower creatures. The man-lion is therefore an embodiment of both power and strength. Not surprisingly, many of the names that originate from the subcontinent symbolize the strength of the lion, or *simha*. For instance, the name Singh originated in India and, in the past, was adopted as a title by certain warrior castes, including the Sikhs. Likewise, the Bihari name Sinha, the Gujarati Sinhji, and the Thai and Sri Lankan Singha all are rooted in the Sanskrit *simha*. Even the name of the southeastern island country of Singapore comes from the Sanskrit Singa Pura, which means Lion City.

There is no paucity of temples dedicated to Narasimha. They are found all over India. Sculptures depicting the man-lion date to the second century CE. A number of prayers have also been written in dedication to this avatar, including the "Narasimha Mahamantra."

> *Faithless is he that says farewell when the road darkens.*
>
> —J.R.R. TOLKIEN, 1892–1973

> *Many of the qualities that come so effortlessly to dogs —loyalty, devotion, selflessness, unflagging optimism, unqualified love—can be elusive to humans.*
>
> —JOHN GROGAN, 1957–

❁ ❁ ❁

7

Avatar #5 – Vamana or Dwarf

If you have been following the advent of avatars sequentially, you might harbor a sneaking suspicion that the supreme gods—Vishnu and Brahma—are often biased and act in favor of *devas* and to the detriment of *asuras*. Your worst fears are about to come true in the Vamana avatar, also known as the dwarf avatar. In this story Vishnu employs cunning and trickery to overthrow an extremely generous and widely respected demon king. Fairness and justice seem to have been ignored. For an outsider, the Hindu divine order may appear rigged, because the demons are destined to fight a losing battle as the supreme gods have already scripted the outcome.

Earlier we saw the demons were victims of a cunning plan that made the gods immortal during the churning of the milky ocean, thanks to the turtle avatar of Vishnu, followed by his gender-bending Mohini avatar. To have any chance of winning against the gods, the demons realized they had to be on equal footing with the gods. This was the situation faced by Bali, a demon king and the grandson of the great Prahlada. He had lost badly to Indra in battle. Like his great grandfather Hiranyakashipu, Bali stood on raised toes with upraised hands to perform severe austerities for many years, and he obtained the boon of conditional immortality. He could lose his immortality only by a curse from Shukra.[15]

Shukra was the chief priest of the demons. He was respected by his peers and had a greater knowledge of the Vedas than his counterpart, Brihaspati, the chief priest of the gods. With Shukra by their side, the demons traditionally outperformed the gods in austerities. So Bali believed that so long as he had the support of Shukra, he should be able to realize his ambition of overthrowing Indra. For Bali, the path to the throne was not difficult, for he was a loyal Vishnu devotee like his grandfather Prahlada. He was also well known for his model conduct and was respected by his peers, superiors, and subordinates alike.

For several years Bali humbly served Shukra, offering devotional service with utmost diligence. Shukra was extremely pleased with his disciple's sincere devotion. With the guidance of his guru, Bali also performed the Vishwajeet *yajna*, a sacrifice that would empower him to become the king of the universe. From the fire arose a golden celestial chariot full of armor and weapons, pulled by white horses, and bearing a flag that displayed a lion. Bali climbed into the chariot and departed with his troops to Indra's capital, Amravati. He was ready to strike and fiercely determined to win the battle.

From afar Indra saw Bali's army advancing toward his city. The enemy soldiers swiftly penetrated the city's fortifications and surrounded the capital. Alarmed, Indra rushed to Brihaspati and sought his advice. After much deliberation Brihaspati told Indra that he was no match for Bali as Shukra had blessed Bali with immense power. Brihaspati instructed the gods to abandon Amaravati, assume other forms, and seek a home elsewhere. Taking his guru's advice, Indra disguised himself as a peacock, while Kubera became a lizard, and the other gods took various covers. Together they headed to the hermitage of Kashyapa. With Indra absent, Bali captured Amravati with ease and declared himself the king of the three worlds.

---

[15] Shukra was the son of the sage Bhrigu, who conducted the test to determine who among the gods was the greatest. This story is described in book 2 of this series.

AVATAR #5 – VAMANA OR DWARF

At the hermitage Kashyapa's wife, Aditi, was deeply perturbed because her mighty son Indra had reduced himself to a peacock. She became indignant for Bali had taken her son's wealth, fame, and even his palace. The bereaved mother of the gods begged Kashyapa to find a way for her son to get his kingdom back. The wise sage asked her to perform the Payovrata, a 12-day fast that required a diet of milk alone, to appease Vishnu. Aditi followed Kashyapa's advice assiduously. She became pregnant and was blessed with a baby boy. But this was no ordinary boy. The boy was short, had matted hair, and carried an umbrella in one hand and a clay water pot in the other. The parents named him Vamana.

Meanwhile Shukra was helping Bali make preparations to perform the Ashvamedha *yajna* with one hundred horses.[16] This was the sacrifice Indra had also performed when he was anointed the king of the universe. A long list of guests, including the dwarf Vamana, was invited for the occasion. When Vamana walked into the sacrifice hall, his divine beauty enchanted everyone present. Although Vamana looked like a child, Bali honored him as a priest and washed his feet. Because it was customary to bestow expensive gifts on the guests, Bali asked the dwarf what he would like. "Dear king, I know generosity flows in your veins. You are lord of the whole world and can give me anything, but my needs are limited. All I ask is some land that I can cover with my three steps," Vamana replied. Bali was humbled by Vamana's restraint. He

The Vamana avatar of Vishnu

---

[16] The Ashvamedha sacrifice is performed to prove a king's sovereignty. In this sacrifice, a sacrificial horse is set loose by a ruler to wander at will for a year. If a neighboring king stops the horse, it means that the king is challenging the ruler. If the neighboring king ignores the horse, it means he accepts the supremacy of the ruler.

was willing to give anything on this occasion, but Vamana wanted only a puny parcel of land. Bali exhorted Vamana to ask something more worthy. But Vamana insisted he wanted only three paces' worth of land.

Nearby, Shukra overheard the conversation and found the request strange. He looked at Vamana and at once felt the radiance within the dwarf. Shukra's suspicion was at once aroused. *This must be Vishnu in disguise,* Shukra thought. Suspecting foul play, he charged at Bali and declared, "Don't give the boy anything! He has come here to help your enemies." Bali was puzzled and protested, "But I have given by word." Shukra urged Bali to renege on his promise, for the priest was certain a trap had been laid. But Bali would not budge. He could not understand why his guru distrusted the innocent boy. "I know, O Master, it is the duty of the householder to protect his wealth, but honoring my word is more important than keeping wealth." With these words Bali poured water on Vamana's hands, signifying that the gift has been given irrevocably. Shukra was irate that the dutiful Bali, who had always served him loyally, had disregarded him this time. Enraged, he cursed Bali, saying, "You did not heed to my advice, so you will suffer the consequences." With that curse, the boon of Bali's invincibility was broken.

Meanwhile, after Bali had acceded to Vamana's request, an incredible thing happened. Vamana began increasing in size until everything in the universe was within his body, including Earth, the other planets, sky, and the oceans. In one stride he straddled the heavens, and in the next he covered Earth. Little did Bali know that Vamana was the fifth incarnation of Vishnu as the Brahmin dwarf. With no place to take his third step, Vamana asked Bali nonchalantly, "Where can I place my third step?" Bali was stumped. "Place your third step on my head," Bali said after some thought. "On your head?" Vishnu asked. "I am less worried about losing my possessions than my honor," Bali replied. With these words he became greater than Vishnu himself. Vishnu smiled and placed his third stride on Bali's head, sending him down to the netherworld. Aditi rejoiced from afar, for her fasting had worked. With Bali banished, her son Indra could take control of the universe.

AVATAR #5 – VAMANA OR DWARF

Recall that the Narasimha avatar showed in no uncertain terms that Vishnu will defend his devotee at any cost. In the Vamana avatar, however, Vishnu appears to have taken a U-turn and abandoned his devotee Bali in favor of Indra. Thus a morally and ethically correct king (Bali) was sidelined for a morally flawed, arrogant former emperor (Indra). Bali clearly was conceited and had extreme ambitions, but his replacement, Indra, was least qualified to succeed Bali. Given the plight of Bali, it may appear that the Hindu divine order is biased or even rigged. But the truth is that Vishnu's fifth avatar was not designed to destroy Bali but to restore the cosmic balance, which had been upset because one had disproportionate power. Bali still remains a powerful king but on a reduced scale. He was not simply stomped to the netherworld; rather, he was sent to Sutala, a realm in the netherworld specially constructed by Vishwakarma, the god of architecture, and supposedly more magnificent than heaven itself. Bali is also celebrated as one of the seven *chiranjeevis*, the distinguished immortals of Hinduism.

While Bali won admiration from Vishnu, he was also the quintessential king among his subjects. Legend has it that Vishnu granted a last wish to Bali that allowed him to visit his subjects once a year. The homecoming of Bali is celebrated every year as the festival of Onam, during which the

Sculpture of Vamana (second from left)
and Rama (at far right) inside Rani Ki Vav, Gujarat, India

Indian state of Kerala pays glorious tribute to the memory of this benign demon. There he is popularly known as Mahabali.[17]

Incidentally, the Vamana avatar is the only Dashavatara that is mentioned in the Vedas. The Rigveda describes Vishnu himself as taking three steps that defined the boundaries of the universe. The gigantic manifestation of Vishnu on this occasion is called Trivikrama, which means "god of three steps." The Vamana avatar is one of the two human avatars (the other is Parashurama) in which Vishnu appears as a Brahmin. The Vamana avatar is also the first time Vishnu appears as a human being.

The shock and awe caused by Vishnu's transformation from a midget to a giant is a common theme of many of his avatars and often referred to as the Trivikrama moment. Recall that both the Matsya and Varaha avatars have their Trivikrama moments in their respective narratives. But the Trivikrama moment has materialized not only in the realm of spirituality but in many spheres of human endeavor. Back in the 1980s, the computer giant IBM invited a young geek called Bill Gates to write software for their new personal computer. The rest is history as Gates not only created the software, but dethroned IBM from the personal computer business.

India has a number of Vamana temples, but most are in South India. The important ones include the Trikkakara Temple (Kochi, Kerala), the Ulagalantha Perumal Temple (Kanchipuram, Tamil Nadu), and the Vamana Temple in the eastern group of temples in Khajuraho, Madhya Pradesh. Ornately carved sculptures of Vamana can be found in many places, including Rani Ki Vav, an 11th-century step well in the town of Patan in Gujarat, India. This site also hosts other Vishnu avatars and was declared a World Heritage Site in 2014. The Indonesian island of Bali is said to have taken its name from this ancient ruler who once was the much loved king of his subjects.

---

[17] The name Mahabali also avoids the confusion with Vali, the monkey king of the Rama avatar. We will meet Vali later in this book.

8

Avatar #6 – Parashurama or Rama with an Axe

> *Aggression only moves in one direction—it creates more aggression.*
> —MARGARET J. WHEATLEY, 1944-

So far the avatars we have discussed came into existence as a result of a demon performing extreme austerities and gaining excessive power that led to a cosmic imbalance. The Parashurama avatar was different. It was rooted in caste conflict in ancient India. Unlike earlier avatars, Parashurama did not occupy his time fighting demons and straightening their roads to dharma. He mostly clashed with the Kshatriyas, members of the Hindu military caste, who had oppressed the Brahmins of that time and sent a chilling warning to unjust kings and rulers that they would suffer reprisals.

In the traditional Hindu caste system, Brahmins comprise the priestly class and Kshatriyas, the warrior class. In ancient times these two upper castes enjoyed a cozy, I'll-scratch-your-back-if-you-scratch-mine relationship. These two castes were dependent on each other and sometimes traded favors with one another. For instance, Kshatriyas needed the sanction of Brahmins to perform rituals, whereas the Brahmins needed the patronage of the Kshatriyas (particularly kings) to secure their legitimacy and livelihood. The situation, however, changed dramatically about the time of the sixth avatar. The warrior class had gained supremacy and dominated the other castes, including the Brahmins. One such despotic Kshatriya ruler was Kartavirya Arjuna.[18] To restore the power of the Brahmins in this caste conflict, Vishnu came into the world as the militant Brahmin Parashurama. Although Parashurama was a Brahmin priest, he had the mind-set of a Kshatriya. When Parashurama was attacked, he did not hurl a curse or hurry to the altar to perform a *yajna*; rather, he returned fire with a more raging fire. Let's get to the story without further ado.

Parashurama was born to the Brahmin sage Jamadagni and his wife, Renuka, as the youngest of five sons. One day when the sons were away in the forest, Renuka went to fetch a pail of water from the river and happened to witness a prince and a damsel entwined in *maithuna*. For a moment she was immersed in unchaste thoughts. When she returned home later than usual, Jamadagni demanded to know what had happened and became enraged on hearing the events. That evening, when his sons returned home one by one from the forest, Jamadagni asked each one to behead his mother. Horrified, the sons flatly refused his orders, thinking their father had gone insane. The sage was infuriated at their disobedience and turned them to stone. The last son to come home was Parashurama. Upon his father's command, he promptly picked up his axe and chopped off his mother's head in a single stroke. Jamadagni was pleased by this youngest son's obedience and granted him a boon. Parashurama at once asked that his mother be restored and his brothers returned to their old selves. From that momentous day the axe became permanently associated with Parashurama. In fact the name Parashu-rama literally means "the axe-wielding Rama." Most texts, however, refer to him

---

[18] Kartavirya Arjuna should not be confused with Arjuna of the Pandava brothers. We discuss Arjuna of the Pandavas in detail in book 4 of this series.

AVATAR #6—PARASHURAMA OR RAMA WITH AN AXE

The sixth avatar, Parashurama, holding an axe and bow

as Parashurama—not Rama—so as not to confuse him with Rama, the seventh avatar of Vishnu. In his incarnation Parashurama truly had an axe to grind—the destruction of Kshatriyas. It was also the axe with which he would later uncover lands—which we will discuss in another chapter.

Stories about the origin of the axe abound. One story[1] relates that Parashurama was a brilliant archer who had shown keen interest in weaponry at an early age. Upon advice by his elders, Parashurama went to the Himalayas and worshipped Shiva for many years. When war broke out between the gods and demons, Shiva asked Parashurama to fight on behalf of the gods and defeat the demons—which he accomplished. In appreciation Shiva not only gave him formidable weapons, such as his signature axe and the Vijaya bow,[19] but also battled-trained him in the use of weapons. Parashurama is also said to have learned Kalaripayattu, the mother of all martial arts, from Shiva.

A seminal event soon took place in Parashurama's life. One day the Kshatriya king Kartavirya Arjuna wandered into the hermitage of Jamadagni while hunting in the forest with his troops. Known to have a thousand arms, Kartavirya was a powerful king who ruled at a time when Brahmins were being violently persecuted by the Kshatriyas. Renuka was alone when the king arrived, but she received him with great deference. At the hermitage the king became curious about Jamadagni's divine cow, Kamadhenu, which produced a sumptuous meal for the king and his troops. The cow was one of the treasures that had emerged during the churning of the milky ocean. The king later gave the cow to Jamadagni as a fee for his services as a priest. In addition to producing bucketsful of full cream milk, the cow also granted any wish. Kartavirya thought that a powerful king like himself should own such a cow and use her to solve the pressing problems of the kingdom. Why should such a cow belong to a hermit living in the forest? He seized the cow despite protests from his hostess, for reclaiming alms was against the code of Hindu dharma.

When Parashurama arrived home that day, he was infuriated to hear what had happened. Jamadagni asked Parashurama to bring the cow back. The obedient son went after the king and soon came face to face with him. A scuffle broke out between the two. Parashurama is said to have clipped the thousand arms of the king, one by one, with his axe, eventually killing him before returning home with the cow. News of Kartavirya's death

---

[19] The Vijaya bow was given to Parashurama by Indra, who had used it to vanquish the demons under the advice of Shiva. After his campaign against the Kshatriyas, Parashurama presented the bow to his famous disciple Karna, a prominent character in the epic Mahabharata.

AVATAR #6–PARASHURAMA OR RAMA WITH AN AXE

reached his sons, who assembled a big army and marched toward the hermitage. When they arrived, Jamadagni was alone there. They wreaked their vengeance on the helpless sage by beheading him.

When Parashurama returned home, his mother told him what had happened. Beating her chest 21 times, she jumped into her husband's funeral pyre and was burned to death. Parashurama, enraged at the double tragedy, vowed to teach the whole of the Kshatriya class a lesson in a language they understood. He led 21 campaigns against them that resulted in the extermination of all the Kshatriya men. It is said that Parashurama killed five generations of warriors and filled five great lakes with their blood. The present generation of Kshatriyas is actually sons of Brahmins born of Kshatriya women.

Allow me to pause for a moment. The stories about Parashurama, as you may have noticed, are different from those of the previous avatars. While the previous stories take place on a superhuman plane, those about Parashurama have a worldly element. He is the first incarnation in which Vishnu appears in a completely human form. The Parashurama avatar occurred during the Treta Yuga, the second of the four yugas, or ages of humanity, in the Hindu cosmic cycle, and his lifetime extended into the third yuga, the Dvapara Yuga, the period of Krishna. Parashurama meets Rama in the Treta Yuga. Parashurama is therefore the only avatar that encountered two other Vishnu avatars in his lifetime.[20] It is a paradox that Parashurama, a Vishnu incarnation, was devoted to Shiva, for Parashurama received all the weapons and training from Shiva.

The Ramayana mentions the meeting of avatars—Parashurama and Rama, the protagonist of the epic Ramayana and the seventh avatar of Vishnu. Before their meeting, Rama had won Princess Sita's hand in marriage at her *swayamvara* by being the only person able to string Pinaka (Shiva's bow). On hearing that Prince Rama had accomplished this feat, Parashurama challenged the Kshatriya prince to prove his mettle by

---

[20] If Balarama is considered an avatar in Dashavataras, then Parashurama has encountered three other Vishnu incarnations in his lifetime.

stringing Vishnu's Sharanga bow.[21] Rama not only strung the Sharanga but placed an arrow in it and pointed it at the challenger's heart. Parashurama was awestruck by the brilliance of Rama. At last Parashurama had found the perfect prince, who not only was strong and valorous but lived by his dharma. The meeting with Rama established Parashurama's trust in kings. After the encounter Parashurama is said to have given up his divine weapons and retired in peace to the Mahendra Mountains.

Although Parashurama is portrayed as an angry, hotheaded, and uncontrollable warrior, many temples in India are dedicated to him. The important ones include the Vadakkunathan Temple (Trissur, Kerala), Parashurama Devalaya (Nanjangud, Karnataka), and Parashurameshwar Mandir (Bhubaneshwar, Orissa). It is said that Parashurama threw his bloodstained axe into the sea, but the sea withdrew in horror, revealing the western India coastlines of Konkan and Malabar. The Puranas state that Parashurama, a devotee of Shiva's, placed statues of Shiva at 108 locations throughout this area—and these can be found even today. For that reason Parashurama is worshipped mostly on the west coast of India.

As one of the seven *chiranjeevis*, the celebrated immortals of Hinduism, Parashurama is believed to be living at his abode in the Mahendra hills, which are often identified as the Eastern Ghats, a range of mountains along India's east coast.

> *Holding on to anger is like grasping a hot coal with the intent of throwing it at someone else; you are the one who gets burned.*
>
> —BUDDHA

---

[21] The wielding of celestial bows is considered an act of immense strength. Major bows in Hindu mythology include Vijaya (Karna), Gandiva (Arjuna), Pinaka and Sharanga. While Brahma created the Gandiva, Vishwakarma crafted the Pinaka and Sharanga for Shiva and Vishnu respectively.

9

Amba Loses Her Honor

He has honor if he holds himself to an ideal of conduct.
—WALTER LIPPMANN, 1889–1974

Now that we have been introduced to Parashurama, we know that he, as the sixth incarnation of Vishnu, was famous for his martial arts skill and expertise in weaponry. We also learned that Parashurama went on a rampage, decimating Kshatriyas, until he met Prince Rama, who made him a changed man and put an end to his slaughter. Scriptures mention another occasion when Parashurama was put to the test during an encounter with an equally powerful warrior, Bhishma, his former student. The battle between the guru and disciple—for protecting Amba's honor—raged for 23 days, five days longer than the Mahabharata War, and separating the combatants required heavenly intervention. Although Parashurama has only a cameo role in the war, the story of Amba is significant because it marked a turning point in the great Mahabharata War. So who's Amba? This tale from the epic Mahabharata is worth telling.

Amba was the oldest daughter of the king of Kasi; her sisters were Ambika and Ambalika. When the girls came of age, the king arranged a *swayamvara* for all three and invited the illustrious monarchs of the region for the occasion. Not invited was the king of nearby Hastinapura. At that time a weakling called Vichitravirya was the head of Hastinapura although the kingdom was actually ruled by his stepbrother Bhishma. As guests arrived at the *swayamvara* from afar, Amba spotted her secret lover, Salva, among the suitors. Unknown to the others, she planned to choose him as her husband. The proceedings came to an unexpected halt when a horse-drawn chariot entered the arena and stopped in front of the princesses. From the chariot came Bhishma, who seized each of the young ladies and put them in his chariot. Before anyone realized what was happening, the chariot drove off with the princesses. As he sped past the arena, Bhishma, confident of his military strength, challenged the invitees: "Come, fight and defeat me or be defeated."

The guests assembled at the arena immediately sent their charioteers in chase. Among them was Salva in his chariot. As they closed in on Bhishma, they faced a torrent of deadly arrows and a horrendous battle followed. With his blazing arrows Bhishma easily knocked down the charioteers and their horses. When the kings realized they were no match for Bhishma, they abandoned their mission and retreated to the safety of their kingdoms. Salva was thrown from his chariot. From the ground he challenged Bhishma to a duel. In the ensuing combat Bhishma wounded Salva but spared his life. After vanquishing all the princes without a scratch on his body, Bhishma headed to Hastinapura and presented the princesses to his stepmother, Satyavati, who made arrangements for their marriage to her son, Vichitravirya. Bhishma had kidnapped the princesses not for himself but for his stepbrother, for Vichitravirya, whose name means "weird seed," was a veritable wimp and could not find a bride for himself even as king of Hastinapura.

As time for the nuptials approached, Ambika and Ambalika succumbed to their destiny and agreed to marry Vichitravirya. Amba, however, confided in Bhishma that she was in love with Salva and had planned to garland him at the *swayamvara*. After consulting with Vichitravirya and Satyavati, Bhishma sent Amba to Salva's palace in a

AMBA LOSES HER HONOR

royal chariot. But Salva had a change of heart. He refused to accept her as his wife because Bhishma had already earned the right to marry her in accordance with Kshatriya dharma. Distraught, Amba went back to Hastinapura and sought refuge there.

The distressed Amba took the desperate measure of asking Vichitravirya to marry her. It was common in those days for kings to have a number of wives. But Vichitravirya refused to accept her because she was in love with someone else. She then begged Bhishma to accept her as his bride. Bhishma reminded her he had taken a vow of celibacy. He was the son of King Shantanu of Hastinapura. In his old age Shantanu had fallen in love with a young fisherwoman called Satyavati and wanted to marry her. The fisherwoman's father, however, stipulated that his daughter's son must inherit the throne. This prenuptial agreement denied the birthright of Bhishma, as the oldest son, to become king. As a devoted son, Bhishma thereupon took a vow that he would never assume the throne or marry or father children.

Amba blamed Bhishma for her misfortune and for tainting her honor by carrying her off. As no man would take her for his wife, she swore to destroy Bhishma. Upon advice from holy men, Amba headed to the Mahendra Mountains and sought Parashurama's help in slaying Bhishma. Initially Parashurama balked at her request because he had taught Bhishma weaponry and warfare. However, on hearing Amba's plight, Parashurama agreed to meet Bhishma. At the meeting Parashurama hollered at Bhishma, "You kidnapped Amba and then later dismissed her. Since you touched her, no other prince will marry her now. She should not have to suffer such humiliation. Therefore, as your former guru, I command you to take her back." But Bhishma was not prepared to take her back. The vow he had taken earlier meant he could not marry. An infuriated Parashurama threatened Bhishma with death and soon they were joined in battle.

The battle went on for 22 days, and both warriors were bloodied and exhausted. On the 23rd day Bhishma attempted to use the deadly divine weapon called Praswapastra against Parashurama. Before Bhishma could release the weapon, the sage Narada appeared and warned him that using the weapon would be a great insult to his guru. Bhishma heeded Narada's advice. Thereafter both combatants disarmed and called off the battle—which was of little comfort to Amba. With a firm resolve she headed to the forest and began performing extreme austerities. She would soon have her ultimate revenge. Reborn as a man, Amba eventually meets her nemesis during the Kurukshetra War, and their encounter becomes the turning point of the battle. But that's another long story, which we describe in book 4 of this series, in the context of the Mahabharata War.

10

Kerala—The Land of Parashurama

Tucked along the southwest coast and Down Under of India is the state of Kerala, which is famous for its lush green fields, serene backwaters, and sun-drenched landscapes. Such is the charm of Kerala that the tropical state is often called "God's own country," particularly by savvy marketing professionals adept in Hindu mythology because two central characters in Dashavataras—Mahabali and Parashurama—have deep connections to Kerala. Legend says that Kerala was formed from the landmass when Parashurama threw his axe into the ocean. Kerala is also the place visited every year by the legendary Mahabali, the *asura* held dear by his people. But that presents a problem: How is it that Parashurama (the sixth avatar) is credited with discovering a place that Mahabali (the demon vanquished by the fifth avatar) was already visiting? [22] Have we just hit upon an inconsistency in the avatar saga?

---

[22] The fifth, sixth, and seventh avatars of Vishnu—namely the Vamana, Parashurama, and the Rama avatars—appeared during the Treta Yuga of the Hindu cosmic cycle.

Not quite. The southwestern coastal areas of Konkan and Malabar—parts of which are within Kerala—existed all along during Mahabali's time. The Puranas say that the western coast of India was once flooded by tumultuous waves and tempests, and Parashurama fought the advancing waters by throwing his bloodstained axe into the sea. Horrified, the water receded from the area, revealing the landmass. Although Parashurama is not in the same league as explorers like Vasco da Gama or Marco Polo, he is credited with discovering Kerala, even though he reclaimed only the coastal belt of Malabar and Konkan with his one act. Recent excavations in these areas and the subsequent discovery of fossils of ancient marine animals from almost all parts of the region confirm that Kerala was once under the sea.

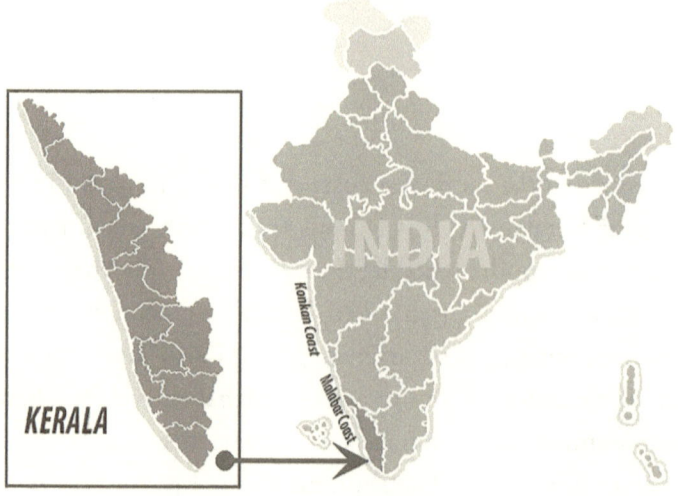

Map of Kerala showing the Konkan and Malabar coastlines

After reclaiming the land, Parashurama is said to have scattered the statues of Shiva—his favorite deity—at 108 locations in this area. That is why Kerala is also known as Parashurama Kshetra, [23] which means "the land of Parashurama." He is said to have invited Brahmins to this region from the north of India. The Brahmins of Kerala, known as Nambudiris,

---

[23] Kshetra means many things, including temple, holy precinct, and land.

consider themselves the most orthodox Brahmins of India and claim to have come to Kerala by walking hand in hand with Parashurama.

Parashurama's love for this land did not stop there. It is believed that he handed down his entire martial arts repertoire—today known as Kalaripayattu—to Kerala families of mixed heritage, that is, those with mothers from the warrior clans and fathers from priestly clans, like, some say, the Nair community in Kerala. Kalaripayattu is often considered the mother of all martial arts, and it has morphed into two major forms, northern and southern versions. The northern Kalari, with its emphasis on weaponry rather than physical combat, is attributed to Parashurama. The southern Kalari, which focuses on weaponless combat, is credited to the sage Agastya. The popularity of Kalaripayattu waned over the years but staged a remarkable comeback in the early 20th century.

The martial art form of Kalaripayattu

Whether Kerala is god's own country is debatable, particularly for people from other Indian states, but there's no denying that Kerala played a significant role in Dashavataras. During his reign Mahabali promoted tolerance and peace and was loved by his subjects. The memory of Mahabali, or his yearly stopovers during Onam, must be what explains the peaceful coexistence of religions, for Kerala is one of the rare states of India where the population is split among Hindus, Christians, and Muslims.

11

Avatar #7 Rama – The One Who Provides Light and Joy

If you are searching for the perfect deity in Hinduism that ticks all the boxes—sincere, dependable, compassionate, courageous, righteous, and intelligent—look no further than Rama. Worshipped by millions of devotees around the world, he is one of the few figures whose fame has lasted thousands of years. Rama is a phenomenon, the quintessential man. Hindus look up to him as Maryada Purushottam, which means the perfect man, and the supreme upholder of dharma. He is held in such high regard that his name has become a popular form of greeting among friends, such as "Ram! Ram!" His name is also invoked at death, for it is considered auspicious to utter his name at the last breath. Many great men from India and elsewhere have been devotees of Rama, including Mahatma Gandhi, whose famous last words were incidentally "Ram Ram."[24]

---

[24] Controversy exists on the last words of Gandhi after he was shot in 1948 by Nathuram Godse at point-blank range. Some say it was "Ram Ram" or "Hey Ram" or even "Ram Rahim." (Rahim is a synonym for the Muslim Allah; Gandhi believed that Rama and Rahim are different names for the same god.) Others believe Gandhi died with a guttural gasp and said nothing.

Let's pause for a moment. Which Rama are we talking about? Okay, in Hinduism there are three renowned Ramas: Parashurama, Balarama,[25] and Ramachandra. The name Rama, which means "he who provides light and joy," is, however, specifically associated with Ramachandra, who manifested as the seventh avatar of Vishnu even while the sixth avatar (Parashurama) was engaged in his mission. The purpose of the Rama avatar was to set things right after the demon king of Lanka, the ten-headed Ravana, became powerful enough to throw the cosmos out of balance. Rama's life is chronicled in the great epic poem Ramayana, which remains one of the most endearing and inspiring stories of all times. In number of verses, Ramayana, at 25,000 verses, is second only to the epic Mahabharata, which boasts of 100,000 verses.

If you think the story of Rama is entirely confined to mythology, you are mistaken. Historically Rama was a member of one of the great dynasties of ancient India, the solar dynasty of Kosala. No one knows exactly when he lived, but it is believed to have been earlier than 3000 BCE. Rama is included in the list of ancient Hindu kings, and at least sixty kings are recorded between Rama and the time of Buddha (ca. 500 BCE). It is plausible that Rama was an ancient king who made a profound impact on his people. Mythology then added color and wings to the story and amplified its magnificence throughout history.

The Ramayana, which means "the travels of Rama," was originally composed by poet Valmiki and is traditionally believed to be the first poem of any kind. That is why Valmiki is considered the first poet. Many versions of Ramayana exist today throughout the length and breadth of India and even outside its perimeter. And in these versions, stories have been added, subtracted, and revised repeatedly over the years. The earliest version, attributed to Valmiki, is known as the Valmiki Ramayana. It was composed between 500 BCE and 200 CE, although the story clearly relates to events that happened during a much earlier period. The story of Rama is also mentioned briefly in the Mahabharata. Rama's popularity

---

[25] Balarama was Krishna's older brother. He is described in book 4 of this series.

AVATAR #7 RAMA–THE ONE WHO PROVIDES LIGHT AND JOY

increased exponentially after the 14th century, when the epics were retold in regional vernaculars. These include Tulsidas's celebrated Hindi version, Ramcharitmanas (The Sacred Lake of the Acts of Rama), and Kamba's Tamil version, Kambaramayana.

The seventh avatar, Rama

RAMA AND THE EARLY AVATARS OF VISHNU

The popularity of Ramayana spread beyond India, particularly after the eighth century, when Indians began to colonize Southeast Asia. Many Asian cultures have adapted the Ramayana, resulting in the creation of many national epics. The Kakawin Rāmâyaṇa, for instance, is a Javanese version of the Sanskrit Ramayana from the ninth-century Indonesia, and it varies little from the original. In the Hikayat Seri Rama of Malaysia, Ravana receives boons from Allah, not Brahma. Thailand's national epic Ramakien is also derived from the Hindu epic, although it adds an element of incest by making Sita the daughter of Ravana. While the main story is identical to that of the Ramayana, many other aspects were fitted to a Thai context, such as the clothes and weapons. An elaborate illustration of Ramakien can be seen at the Wat Phra Kaew Temple in Bangkok. Adaptations of Ramayana can also be found in Laos, the Philippines, Cambodia, and Myanmar, where locals incorporated their history, folklore, and religious beliefs to make the epic relevant to that region.

India has many temples dedicated to Rama. The image of Rama is often accompanied by his wife Sita, brother Lakshmana, and his assistant Hanuman kneeling at his feet. In paintings Rama is depicted dark in color—which is a common feature of all Vishnu avatars. Worship of Rama, however, is not restricted to temples. Every year Rama's exemplary life is celebrated in a drama called Rama Lila with young children reenacting the key episodes of the Ramayana. The performances often last more than one week and culminate with the death of Ravana on the day of Dussehra,[26] followed by Rama's coronation the next day. Rama's birth is also celebrated with the festival Rama Navami on his birthday. The most widely observed festival, however, is Diwali, the festival of lights.[27] Diwali commemorates the return of Rama, with Sita and Lakshmana, from his 14-year exile. It is believed that the people of Ayodhya, the capital of Rama's kingdom, celebrated the occasion by illuminating the

---

[26] Dussehra is a festival that celebrates the triumph of good over evil. It is usually celebrated on the tenth and final day of the Hindu festival of Navaratri.

[27] Diwali is also celebrated in honor of the goddess Lakshmi.

AVATAR #7 RAMA–THE ONE WHO PROVIDES LIGHT AND JOY

Hanuman, with (from left to right) Rama, Sita, and Lakshmana

city with earthen oil lamps and setting off firecrackers.

Just as Rama is seen as the perfect man, his wife is regarded as the perfect woman, or *pativrita*, and together they form the ideal Hindu couple and perfect role model for many Indians. The Maryada Purushottam Rama is courteous even to his enemies. When Rama came face to face with his archrival Ravana for the first time, it is said that Rama approached him with folded hands and said, "I bow to you, O Master of the Vedas." Ravana presumed this act was a sign of weakness and replied, "Are you afraid to face me in battle?" To which Rama replied, "You are a Brahmin, and you are wise and knowledgeable. Courtesy dictates that I respect you for your abilities. Together we have come to the battlefield for a purpose. We will fulfill that." After the meeting Ravana is said to have told his wife: "My nemesis is not only an expert in archery, he speaks convincingly too."

As a testament to his truthfulness and courage, Rama is the inspiration behind common names like Raghava, Pattabhirama, Ramadasa, and Vijayaraghava. We next turn our attention to the epic Ramayana.

Contrary to popular belief, the epic shows that Rama is human after all in spite of being draped in an avatar, and the ending is not the fairy tale you would expect.

> *Man will ever remain imperfect,*
> *and it will always be his part to try to be perfect.*
>
> —MAHATMA GANDHI, 1869–1948

❖ ❖ ❖

12

The Story of Rama – 1

In the next three chapters, we narrate the story of Ramayana. The Valmiki Ramayana consists of seven sections. This chapter summarizes roughly the first three sections, the "Bala Kanda," "Ayodhya Kanda," and "Aranya Kanda."

Dashanana is not the garden variety villain of Hindu mythology. Born as a Brahmin, Dashanana was well known for his mastery of the Vedas. He was considered the most distinguished devotee of Shiva's. He was a formidable warrior, as well as an able administrator, an expert in astrology, and an accomplished musician. Unfortunately not many people know Dashanana. But when referred to by his other name, Ravana, most people at once recognize him as the greatest villain of Hinduism. (Shiva coined the name Ravana to reflect Dashanana's bloodcurdling screams.) Despite having a long list of virtues, Ravana became the prime adversary and villain in the Ramayana. He was a serial rapist, perhaps the first to start abducting women in ancient times. The brunt of his wickedness was borne by his stepbrother Kubera from whom Ravana stole his palace in Lanka and his famous aerial chariot. The pivotal moment in the Ramayana, however, belongs not to the hero or the villain but to a lowly maid servant called Manthara, who sets the prince of Kosala, Rama, on a collision course with the most heinous demon Hinduism has ever witnessed. Let us rewind and start from the beginning.

King Dasharatha, a descendant of the illustrious solar dynasty of kings, was an impartial ruler of Kosala and loved his subjects as if they were his own children. He was married to Kausalya, but they were childless for a number of years. He married again, to Sumitra, and then again to Kaikeyi, until he realized he needed a different approach to cure his childlessness. Dasharatha desperately wanted to beget an heir to his throne. It was customary in those times to perform austerities to accomplish major goals. So Dasharatha started practicing *tapas* in the hope of getting his wish fulfilled.

About that time, the gods were in great distress because of the deeds and threats of Ravana, the ten-headed demon king of Lanka. No ordinary demon, Ravana was the commander of rakshasas, a genre of fierce-looking demons who practiced cannibalism. Like the demons Hiranyaksha and Hiranyakashipu, Ravana undertook severe austerities to appease Brahma, who granted him immunity from being killed by gods, demons, or Gandharvas.[28] Ravana also was careful to appease Shiva and obtain his blessings. Although Ravana's power increased exponentially with the boons, his morality grew in inverse proportion to the power.[29] With his almost unlimited powers, Ravana showed his demonic hues by persecuting gods and humans. Distraught, the gods gathered and discussed how to stop this powerful demon. After much thought, they decided Vishnu should take the form of a human, for Ravana had been too proud to ask for immunity from humans. But Ravana was a powerful figure and a faithful devotee of Shiva's, so even a god of Vishnu's stature could not overcome the

---

[28] Gandharvas are male nature spirits who act as messengers between gods and humans. They are considered the husbands of *apsaras* and are known for their musical skills.

[29] The 19th-century British historian Lord Acton first observed that morality is inversely proportional to power.

demon without outside help. The other gods agreed to help Vishnu either by assuming various forms or by lending their powers to humans or animals. A concerted effort was thus planned to thwart the threat of Ravana.

Back at Kosala, many years of austerities failed to fulfil Dasharatha's wish for an heir. At last Dasharatha performed the Putrakameshti sacrifice, the most a king could do to please the gods for the sake of having a son. This time the fire god Agni emerged from the sacrificial fire and gave him a magic pudding to share among his wives. Dasharatha gave half the pudding to Kausalya, his principal queen, a quarter to Sumitra, and the remaining quarter to Kaikeyi. Four sons were born as a result. Kausalya gave birth to the oldest Ramachandra (Rama), who was born with a half of the divine essence. Kaikeyi gave birth to Bharata, who was similarly endowed with a quarter of divinity. Sumitra bore twins Lakshmana and Shatrughna, who each had an eighth of the divine essence. Thus the incarnation was divided among four mortals for this colossal task.

The four brothers grew up together at Ayodhya, the capital of Kosala, and learned archery at a young age. The brothers were all attached to one another, but from childhood, Rama and Lakshmana were inseparable companions. Once the sage Vishwamitra visited Ayodhya and sought Rama's help. The sage needed protection from the rakshasas, who were harassing the hermits of that region by disrupting their *yajnas*. Dasharatha was at first unwilling to send Rama because he was still young, but the king reluctantly acceded to the sage's request and sent Rama along with Lakshmana to help the sage. Shortly thereafter Rama encountered the mighty rakshasa called Tadaka, who had the strength of a thousand elephants and terrorized the region. Initially Rama had some reservations about killing Tadaka because she was a woman, so he chopped off her hands. Using her demonic powers, Tadaka, however, became invisible and continued her attack, this time targeting the brothers. Rama eventually killed her by shooting an arrow into her heart. With Tadaka annihilated, the rest of the rakshasas did not have a chance against the brothers. Vishwamitra was pleased and presented Rama with a cache of celestial arms—and these would become useful in the future.

While the princes were roaming the forest, they heard that King Janaka had arranged a *swayamvara* for his beautiful daughter, Sita. No ordinary girl, she was believed to be an incarnation of the goddess Lakshmi herself. She was born of Mother Earth and adopted by the king after he found her in the furrow of a rice paddy. For Sita's *swayamvara* the challenge was to string Pinaka, the mighty bow of Shiva, and shoot an arrow from it. None of the suitors could lift the bow, let alone string it. Several months had passed and the bow remained unstrung. Vishwamitra ushered the young princes to Janaka's court, where the bow was displayed. Rama walked across the assembly hall, picked up the bow, and strung it nonchalantly. He then plucked the bowstring and it twanged so loudly that the sound thundered in the nearby forest. The sheer force broke the bow in two. Janaka and his courtiers were overjoyed to see Rama win the hand of the princess. Rama married Sita and they proceeded to Ayodhya, where he was enthusiastically received by Dasharatha and the people.

After Rama's marriage to Sita, Dasharatha realized he was becoming feeble with old age and decided to install Rama on the throne. Preparations were made at Ayodhya for the coronation of Rama as his successor. The whole country rejoiced at the announcement except Manthara. A wicked hunchback, Manthara served in the royal quarters as a maid servant to Kaikeyi, the third and youngest wife of Dasharatha. On the eve of Rama's coronation, Manthara fanned the flames of jealousy in Kaikeyi by reminding her of the king's promise to her. At the time of Kaikeyi's wedding, the king had promised Kaikeyi that her son would succeed him on the throne. The maid's words aroused in Kaikeyi a strong resentment of Rama. Kaikeyi met with Dasharatha and complained about the injustice. She reminded him of the two boons he had given her in the past. Many years earlier, when Dasharatha was waging a fierce battle with a demon, Dasharatha's chariot lost one of its wheel pins. Kaikeyi, who was with him in the chariot, put her little finger in the pinhole and kept the wheel in place, thereby saving her husband's life. Now Kaikeyi wanted Dasharatha to fulfill her boons. She asked Dasharatha to make her son Bharata the king and exile Rama for fourteen years in the forests of Dandaka.

Rama breaking the bow at the *swayamvara*, 19th-century painting by Raja Ravi Varma

Dasharatha was overcome with grief. Unable to go back on his word, he sequestered himself in a room of his palace. Meanwhile Kaikeyi told Rama what had happened between her and the king. As a dutiful son, Rama willingly agreed to go into exile. He then broke the news to Sita. Although Rama told Sita about the difficulties of forest life, she insisted on accompanying him. Just as the devoted Savitri had followed her husband, Satyavan, even after his death, Sita wanted to be with her husband in good times and bad.[30] Nor could Lakshmana remain separated from

---

[30] See book 1 of this series for the story of Satyavan and Savitri.

his favorite brother. So he decided to accompany the couple. Together the three departed for the forests amid the grief-stricken populace. An occasion that was meant for rejoicing had turned into mourning.

A week after Rama left for the forest, Dasharatha died of grief. Bharata and Shatrughna had been at their maternal grandfather's palace when these unfortunate events unfolded at Ayodhya. When they heard that Rama had left, they rushed to Ayodhya, where they learned that their father had died of grief. Bharata was angry at his mother's conduct and blamed her for his father's death. His brother Shatrughna dragged Manthara from her servant's quarters and attempted to kill her, but he was restrained by Bharata, who believed Rama would never approve of such conduct. Bharata declined to ascend the throne and then set out with an army to bring Rama back from the forest.

Meanwhile Rama was camping at the Chitrakuta Hills when he saw clouds of dust in the distance. As the sound of an army became louder, Lakshmana climbed a tree to get a glimpse of the approaching army. Lakshmana thought hostilities were about to resume and became worried. But Bharata halted his army at a distance and approached alone. He threw himself at Rama's feet, but the older brother lifted him and they embraced. Bharata informed Rama about their father's death and implored him to come back to Ayodhya. But Rama refused to return, stating that it was his duty to honor his father's last wish. A despondent Bharata returned to Ayodhya with a pair of Rama's sandals, which he kept on the throne as a symbol of Rama, and ruled the kingdom as his proxy.

After the encounter, Rama moved farther south into the deeper regions of the forest so that the people of Ayodhya could not find him. He spent ten years of his banishment by moving from one hermitage to another. During his sojourn he also visited the hermitage of Agastya near the Vindhya Mountains. On Agastya's advice Rama went to live in a place called Panchavati on the banks of the river Godavari. The area was infested with rakshasas, and one of them, Shurpanakha, the sister of Ravana, fell in love with the handsome prince at first sight. She changed her form into that of a young girl and tried to seduce Rama, but he rejected her overtures by reminding her that he was already married. He suggested that Lakshmana might be interested. When Lakshmana also resisted her advances, Shurpanakha attacked Sita in a fit of jealousy and tried to devour her. An enraged Lakshmana went after the demoness and cut off her nose and ears. In retaliation Shurpanakha called upon her younger brother Khara to attack Rama. An army of rakshasas led by Khara marched toward Rama and attacked him. But they were no match for the brothers and the rakshasas were clobbered. Khara died in the encounter.

With the loss of her brother, Shurpanakha became even more desperate for revenge. She sought vengeance through her older brother, Ravana. She was aware of Ravana's weakness for women and told him that Sita was an incomparable beauty and would be a wonderful addition to his harem. The very mention of a beautiful lady made Ravana excited, but he realized that this was easier said than done, for Rama was a formidable opponent. The only way to get to Sita was through trickery and deceit. So he hatched a plot to abduct Sita. Ravana enlisted the services of his ally Maricha, whom he asked to become a golden deer. He then sent Maricha to graze near the clearing where Sita lived. On seeing the beautiful deer, Sita asked Rama to capture the animal for her. Rama tried to trap the deer, but the deer was too fast for him. He then shot the deer down with an arrow. To his surprise, Rama heard the wounded animal crying and mimicking his voice, saying, "O Sita, O Lakshmana" as though Rama himself was in danger. When Sita heard the helpless cries from afar, she asked Lakshmana to find out what had happened to her husband. Lakshmana was hesitant to leave Sita alone in the hermitage. He drew a circle in the sand—the famed Lakshmana Rekha[31]—and told Sita she would be safe so long as she did not leave this circle.

While Lakshmana was away, Ravana, who had been observing the situation hidden behind a bush, approached Sita in the garb of an old mendicant and begged for alms. As the unsuspecting Sita took pity on

---

[31] Today Lakshmana Rekha refers to a strict convention or rule, the violation of which may lead to grave consequences.

him and stepped outside the circle, the mendicant turned into his true self. Sita cried for help, but Ravana seized her by her arms and dragged her into his aerial chariot. Before anyone knew what was happening, the ten-headed Ravana had stolen Rama's wife and headed off to his palace in Lanka.

The story continues in the next chapter.

Ravana visits Sita disguised as a mendicant, 19th-century painting by Raja Ravi Varma

13

The Story of Rama—II

This chapter covers the fourth and fifth sections of the Valmiki Ramayana, namely the "Kishkindha Kanda" and the "Sundara Kanda."

At nearly 25,000 verses, the Ramayana is a thick book, about six times the thickness of this one. The plot is also thick. When we last saw Sita, she had been abducted by Ravana and was aboard his flying chariot on his way to his capital, Lanka. Let us continue the story from here.

The abduction of Sita did not go completely unnoticed. As Ravana maneuvered his chariot through the skies, he saw a large bird flying menacingly toward him. It was Jatayu, the vulture king, who intercepted Ravana in the skies and blocked the chariot's course with its wings. The powerful bird fought the demon with its talons and beak. Unable to break free from the bird, Ravana eventually unleashed his sword and cut off the bird's wings. With its wings chopped off, Jatayu could no longer remain airborne. It plunged to earth, landing fatally wounded. A relieved Ravana steadied his chariot and continued his journey toward Lanka. On reaching Lanka, Ravana dragged Sita to his quarters. He tried to woo her with soothing words, but she rejected his advances. Incensed, Ravana raised his sword, threatening to kill her, but she was saved by the timely intervention of Mandodari, Ravana's queen.

Ravana clips the vulture Jatayu's wings, 19th-century painting by Raja Ravi Varma

Meanwhile Rama's despair and rage at the loss of his wife was beyond words. After a lengthy search for Sita, Rama and Lakshmana found Jatayu lying in a pool of blood. The bird told them about its encounter with Ravana. That was when they learned of Sita's fate and realized they were victims of a cruel plot. After cremating Jatayu's body, the princes continued their search for Sita and entered the kingdom of monkeys called

Kishkindha, located south of Kosala. They met the deposed king Sugriva and his trusted lieutenant Hanuman. When the princes inquired about Sita, the monkeys showed them some ornaments that belonged to Sita. They had seen a beautiful lady crying and dropping her ornaments from a chariot in the sky that was heading south and driven by a demon. Rama was sad and tearful upon learning of Sita's whereabouts.

But Rama realized that Ravana had a commanding army, so he needed an equally strong army to rescue Sita from captivity. So he entered into an alliance with the monkey king Sugriva, who promised to assist Rama on the condition that the prince help Sugriva regain his kingdom. Sugriva's older brother Vali had banished Sugriva from the kingdom while holding Sugriva's wife captive in his palace. But vanquishing Vali in combat was not an easy task. Many years earlier Vali had performed severe penances and pleased Brahma, who bestowed on Vali a peculiar boon: anyone who fought him one on one in combat would lose half his strength to Vali. The boon made it difficult to prevail against Vali.

Together Rama and Sugriva sought out Vali. Sugriva dared Vali to fight and charged at him, but Vali held him back. Rama watched from afar. The brothers were evenly matched and indistinguishable in battle. They fought with fists, stones, trees, nails, and teeth until Hanuman placed a garland of flowers around Sugriva's neck. The garland allowed Rama to identify Sugriva from afar. Concealed behind a tree, Rama shot an arrow straight at Vali's heart, mortally wounding him. After Sugriva was restored to the throne, he honored his promise and raised a huge army of monkeys and bears and marched toward Lanka with Rama and Lakshmana.

They reached the southern tip of the land and came to a complete halt. The sea separated Lanka from the mainland, offering a natural protection from invasion. Rama decided to construct a bridge over the waters with assistance from the army of monkeys. The monkeys felled trees and collected logs and giant boulders. They began constructing a floating bridge by tossing the stones into the water. According to the legend, the stones did not sink because they had Rama's name written on them. It was then Rama realized that Hanuman was no ordinary monkey. Hanuman could leap and fly long distances. While the construction of the bridge was in progress, Hanuman flew over the sea to Lanka on a reconnaissance mission. Undetected by guards, he entered Ravana's pleasure garden, where he found Sita, sad and lonely, under a tree surrounded by rakshasa guards. The monkey climbed a tree without the guards' knowledge and began chanting songs in praise of Rama. On hearing the name of her lord, Sita looked up and saw Hanuman, who gestured to her that he was a friend. He told her about the rescue operations in progress and gave Rama's signet ring to her as a token of his love.

Delighted with his success, Hanuman decided to celebrate with some monkey mischief and frolicked in Ravana's garden, destroying the

Hanuman sets Lanka on fire with his burning tail, 19th-century painting by Raja Ravi Varma

king's favorite plants and flowers. He was soon caught by the rakshasas and brought before Ravana. Still buoyant, Hanuman raised himself by coiling his tail so that he was seated higher than the king. The enraged Ravana was about to kill him, but Vibhishana, Ravana's youngest brother, intervened and told Ravana that Hanuman was an envoy and therefore qualified for diplomatic immunity. Nevertheless Ravana wanted to teach him a lesson and ordered his soldiers to set his tail on fire. As his tail burned, Hanuman leaped from building to building, thereby setting the whole of Lanka on fire.

Hanuman then flew back to the mainland and gave strategic information about Ravana's defenses to Rama. Lanka was a mighty fortress, for it had been built by Vishwakarma for Kubera, the god of wealth, from whom Ravana had stolen it. Originally Lanka was located at the summit of Mount Meru. Upon Narada's advice Vayu, the wind god, blew Lanka from the top of the mountain and hurled it into the sea, where it later became the island of Lanka.[32]

Meanwhile at the palace in Lanka, Vibhishana tried to save Sita's life. Although he was a rakshasa himself, Vibhishana was of a noble character and pressed Ravana to return Sita to her husband. Ravana was not pleased to hear such advice from Vibhishana and told him to leave the kingdom. Vibhishana left the palace and magically flew to Rama's camp, where he sought asylum. Rama welcomed him wholeheartedly, and together they devised the battle plan. Vibhishana told Rama that Ravana's army was made up of millions of demons. He also told Rama that Ravana's son Indrajit possessed great magical powers and would be a daunting opponent.

Shortly after Hanuman's return, the bridge—known as Rama's Bridge—was completed. With this critical piece of infrastructure in place, Rama was ready, with his motley army of monkeys, to set foot on Lanka and confront Ravana.

---

[32] The mythological origin of Lanka is described in book 1 of this series.

14

The Story of Rama—III

This chapter addresses the sixth and final sections of the Valmiki Ramayana—the "Yuddha Kanda" and the "Uttara Kanda."

By nightfall the princes, Hanuman, and the monkey army had crossed the bridge to Lanka. As they entered the island, some cheered by shouting, "Victory to Rama!" Shortly thereafter a mighty battle began between the armies of Rama and Ravana at the gates of Lanka. Ravana's forces included his formidable son Indrajit. Originally called Meghanada, he once had defeated Indra and earned the title Indrajit, or conqueror of Indra. To obtain Indra's freedom at that time, Brahma negotiated with Meghanada and gave him the boon of near immortality. Now Indrajit showed his military skills against Rama in no uncertain terms. His weapons landed on monkeys with precision and took an enormous toll on them. Next he hurled a powerful weapon at Lakshmana and impaled him. Lakshmana fell to the ground unconscious. With Lakshmana near death, Hanuman was called upon to fetch the magical herb Sanjeevani from the Himalayas. Only this herb could save Lakshmana's life.

Hanuman immediately flew all the way to the Himalayas.[33] On reaching the mountains, he had difficulty identifying the herb. So he decided to lift the entire mountain and bring it to the battleground. After a thorough search, the herb was found and Lakshmana was saved from death. Meanwhile Ravana's younger brother Kumbhakarna, a good-natured giant who sleeps for six months and has a voracious appetite, caught monkeys by the hundreds and devoured them. But the monkeys who were spared pressed hard and inflicted heavy losses on the rakshasas. In an attempt to create divisions in Rama's army, Ravana told the monkeys that Rama considered them lowly, expendable animals. However, the faithful monkeys dismissed Ravana's claims and continued to fight with gusto. With his remarkable strength Hanuman smashed the skull of every enemy he encountered. Seeing Hanuman's great courage, the monkey army rallied behind their leader and fought harder. Finally they killed Meghanada, Kumbhakarna, and other rakshasa generals, and the battle came down to Rama and Ravana, face-to-face.

The earth trembled as the whole company of gods watched the fight. The air was thick with arrows flying in both directions. Both Rama and Ravana were masters of the bow and arrow. Rama struck off Ravana's head with several arrows in succession, but as each head fell, another one grew in its place. The battle went on for days. Finally Rama drew forth the magical weapon Brahmastra, which the sage Agastya had given him. Believed to be one of the most destructive weapons, Brahmastra, when discharged, can be stopped only by another Brahmastra. Chanting mantras, Rama aimed at Ravana and let loose the arrow. It whizzed through the air emitting flames and pierced the heart of Ravana, who fell to the ground with a murderous cry. Ravana's end was so abrupt and final that

---

[33] The magical Sanjeevani is said to have the power to cure any malady. No one knows what plant this was, and several plants have been proposed as candidates, including *Selaginella bryopteris*, an herb used in traditional Indian medicine to treat a range of disorders; *Dendrobium plicatile*, an Asian orchid; and *Cressa cretica*, a flowering plant in the morning glory family. The search for Sanjeevani is being undertaken by various state governments of India even today.

no one could believe their eyes. There was great rejoicing among the gods, who showered Rama with garlands and then resurrected the monkeys that had fallen in battle.

Although Ravana had been a terror in the region, he was given a proper funeral and his body cremated according to Vedic rituals. Vibhishana was

Hanuman fetching the herb-bearing mountain, 20th-century painting, artist unknown

appointed the king of Lanka. The news of Rama's victory reached Sita. She was overjoyed and arrived in a palanquin to meet Rama. But, to the shock of all, Rama was cold toward her and refused to look at her. He could no longer accept his wife because she had been looked upon with lustful eyes by another. Sita was humiliated and protested her unfailing love for him. But Rama doubted Sita had been able to preserve her virtue as Ravana's captive. So he asked Sita to prove her chastity by undergoing the Agni Pariksha, or trial by fire. Agni Pariksha is an ancient practice that requires a woman to walk through a blazing pyre. If the woman emerges unscathed, she is said to be chaste. Many, including Lakshmana, protested Rama's decision, although Lakshmana eventually lighted the pyre. Determined to prove her chastity, Sita submitted herself to the scorching flames and came through them unharmed, proving her purity to everyone. After the test Rama accepted her wholeheartedly, saying that he had never doubted her purity but required the test for public proof. Yet the question of chastity did not completely disappear from their lives.

By now the term of exile for Rama was over. With Sita, Lakshmana, and other monkey generals, Rama proceeded to Ayodhya, where he was crowned king. The country enjoyed unprecedented peace and prosperity for many years. The question of chastity reared its ugly head again when a *dhobi* in the kingdom beat his wife, whom he suspected of adultery. He told his wife that he was not a fool like Rama and did not believe that a wife kept for years by another man was pure. Soon murmurs and whispers expressing doubts about Sita's innocence spread through the kingdom. As a king and the epitome of dharma, Rama was expected to uphold moral principles and maintain his dynasty's reputation. To save Sita and himself from further slander, Rama sent her away to the forest, even though she was pregnant at the time. Many devotees of Rama felt he was wrong to forsake Sita, especially since she had proved her purity.

In the forest Sita found shelter in Valmiki's hermitage. With Sita out of the kingdom, the rumors died down. Shortly thereafter and unknown to Rama, Sita gave birth to twin boys, Lava and Kusha, in the hermitage.[34] As time passed, Rama and Sita became accustomed to living apart in different parts of the country. Years later Rama planned to extend his sovereignty and performed the Ashvamedha sacrifice in which a ceremonial horse was allowed to wander at will. The horse circled the whole country without being challenged, but on its return journey two boys stopped the equine in the forest. Blocking the path of the horse was considered an act of defiance against the king. In catching the horse, they boldly challenged the authority of Rama himself.

As the news reached the capital, Rama sent Lakshmana to arrest the boys. Surprisingly Lakshmana proved no match and was summarily defeated. Bharata and Shatrughna followed Lakshmana—but they met the same fate. Astounded, Rama sent Hanuman to teach the boys a lesson. Even the powerful Hanuman did not prevail, for he was subdued by the boys and tied up with ropes. Eventually Rama himself arrived at the scene and soon entered battle against the boys. Midway through the fight Rama realized he was up against a pair of tenacious boys, whose courage and strength were second to none. Valmiki was watching the turn of events from the sidelines. He could no longer remain passive and intervened to end the fight. The sage revealed to Rama that the boys were none other than his illustrious sons, Lava and Kusha. On seeing his family, Rama was overpowered by love and nostalgia. He invited Sita and his sons back to his palace.

The family was soon reunited in Ayodhya. Yet the issue of chastity lingered. Sita was asked to prove her innocence a second time before a court of people. Sita realized there would be no end to this ordeal. In protest, she called upon Earth, her mother, to take her back. Soon a rift opened in the ground beneath her and Sita disappeared into it. Thus Rama lost his one and only beloved wife forever. Rama was heartbroken and wished to follow her. He proceeded to the banks of the river Sarayu. Walking into the water, he was hailed by Brahma and transported to Vishnu's abode.

---

[34] The city of Lahore in Pakistan gets its name from Prince Lava.

> *An entire sea of water cannot sink a ship unless it gets inside the ship. Similarly, the negativity of the world cannot put you down unless you allow it to get inside you.*
>
> —ANONYMOUS

❋ ❋ ❋

15

Is Rama the Perfect Man?

There are no perfect men in this world, only perfect intentions.

—PEN DENSHAM, 1947–

What kind of man is your partner? Is he the type who accepts you the way you are? Does he stand by you in lean and hard times? Does he bend the rules for you? Does he have a large heart, so big that you fear he can accommodate many like you? If this sounds like your spouse, he fits the description of a Krishna-type lover. Or are you committed to someone who is utterly dedicated to you? Are you his only love? Has he no room for another woman in his heart? If so, he is the perfect man, so perfect that he demands the same perfection from you in the way society perceives you. If this sounds more like your man, he is a Rama-like lover. Famous men like Gandhi and Obama are the quintessential Rama types—reliable but driven by ideology. Nehru and Kennedy, on the contrary, were the Krishna[35] types—practical but not perfect. Most women, however, believe their partners are neither Rama nor Krishna but

---

[35] Krishna is described in book 4 of this series.

bear some of the traits of Ravana. Most men are, however, likely to start out as Rama, turn into Krishna, and a few into Ravana, and eventually become Shiva.

Rama is considered the perfect man in the Hindu culture. He is the supreme upholder of dharma and known as Maryada Purushottam. In the Valmiki Ramayana, Rama is surrounded by a throng of idealistic people; for example, a wife who would live and die in his shadow, a brother who would not accept kingship, and a father who would rather die than break his promise. Throughout, the epic espouses and upholds the traditional values of Hindu society, such as religious duty (dharma), social hierarchy (*varna*), and stages of life (*ashrama*). Rama is the epitome of all these values. While Krishna often challenges accepted social norms, Rama is a pillar of Hindu society and upholds its values. As a model of the perfect son, he shows his devotion to his parents by attaching more importance to his duties as a son than as a husband. Although Krishna had multiple relationships with his female devotees in the name of divine play, Rama is monogamous and dedicated to his wife, Sita. In battle he's the fiercest of the combatants and symbolizes the warrior ideal of using strength to uphold justice, protect the virtuous, and vanquish the wicked. The qualities of Rama resonate with some of the most deeply cherished values of Hindu culture.

Did Rama truly live up to his role as the Maryada Purushottam in the entire 25,000 verses of the Valmiki Ramayana? Is he all virtue and goodness to the bone? One would mostly say yes, but few events in the epic are troubling as they portray Rama as stepping out of character when tensions rise. For instance, Rama violates the notion of fair and honorable warfare when he shoots Vali in the back from a concealed place in an attempt to assist the monkey king Sugriva. But, then, Vali was the possessor of a peculiar boon that meant anyone who fought him one on one lost half his strength to Vali—which made him invincible. Even Ravana fought and lost to Vali because of this boon.

The Valmiki Ramayana further corroborates the rigidity and oppressiveness of the caste structure in existence at that time. To uphold the

IS RAMA THE PERFECT MAN?

Rama and Sita

social order, Rama slew a low-caste Shudra called Shambuka whom he found practicing penances, which was a violation of his dharma because such privilege was reserved for the upper castes. The ideal Hindu society—or Ramaraj, as it is often referred to—was based on the four-class caste system, and, as the king, Rama was bound to uphold the class hierarchy.[36] Thus it was his duty to kill Shambuka, who had transgressed his class and wanted to be a Brahmin. The epic describes another scene in which Rama had molten lead poured into the ears of another Shudra who had been caught listening to the Vedas. Violation of the caste dharma was a grave

---

[36] See book 1 for a detailed exploration of the caste system.

offense in those days. The Manusmriti prescribes heavy sentences, such as cutting the tongue, or pouring molten lead in the ears, of offenders who recite or listen to the Vedas. Today the Shambuka episode, however, is often used to highlight the oppressiveness of Hinduism's caste system. Although dharma was the ultimate goal of the Valmiki Ramayana, the later versions of the Ramayana, such as the Ramcharitmanas by Tulsidas, emphasize bhakti (devotion) in addition to dharma.

If Rama can be excused for killing Vali from a hidden place because of Vali's special boon, he can also be condoned for mutilating Shurpanakha, Ravana's sister, to save Sita from Shurpanakha's attack. Recall Shurpanakha met Rama in the forest and was instantly smitten by his winsome looks. Rama, however, turned down her overtures by pointing out that he was already married. Out of courtesy, he then suggested to the demoness that Lakshmana might be interested in her. When Lakshmana also resisted her affection, Shurpanakha attacked Sita out of jealousy and tried to devour her. An enraged Lakshmana went after Shurpanakha and cut off her nose and ears. Some texts state that Rama also participated in the mutilation. These actions, however, seem incompatible with the Kshatriya ethic of respect for women and the righteous use of force.

Perhaps the most unsettling issue in the Ramayana is Rama's treatment of his wife. Immediately after she was liberated from Ravana's captivity, Rama forced her to undertake an Agni Pariksha. Although Sita emerged unscathed from the fire ordeal and proved her claim that she had remained chaste during captivity, Rama abandoned her when she was pregnant. When the family reunited after several years, Rama insisted on an additional test at which Sita protested and was swallowed up by the earth. Rama's character therefore remains somewhat tarnished because of his attitude toward his wife, yet he cannot be dismissed as a bad husband. Buddha, for instance, is not known to be a lousy husband even though he abandoned his wife and infant to seek his own spiritual path.

In the final analysis, the central theme and substance of the Ramayana is the love of Rama and his lawfully wedded wife. The love between them is also a love in harmony with dharma. The portrayal of Rama conveyed by the epic is of a character who is righteous by the standards of his time but would at times be considered rigid and inflexible today. This depiction of Rama, however, is limited because we have few sources that describe him. Accounts of Krishna appear in many places other than the Mahabharata, but there is not much literature on Rama apart from the Ramayana or its manifold versions.[37] Thus all our value judgements are based on the exposition of one text, the Ramayana.

> *Men are like wine—some turn to vinegar,*
> *but the best improve with age.*
>
> —POPE JOHN XXIII, 1881–1963

---

[37] Other limited descriptions of Rama appear in Vishnu Purana and Bhagavata Purana, both of which were written after the Valmiki Ramayana.

16

Ravana – The Greatest Villain of Hinduism

The Hindu festival Dussehra celebrates the triumph of Rama over the ten-headed demon king Ravana, who seized Rama's wife without her consent and held her captive in Lanka. Symbolizing the victory of justice over injustice, the festival is marked by parades and fanfare where effigies of the bad guy Ravana are stuffed with firecrackers and set ablaze at night. That said, if Ravana is the ultimate villain of Hinduism, how come temples dedicated to him exist even today when places of worship barely exist for celebrated gods like Indra, Varuna and Brahma?

This takes us back to the point that the bad guy in Hindu culture is not painted in just two colors, black or white. That is, *bad* does not translate to "100 percent bad," just as a good guy may not be good all the time. Both have infinite shades of gray between them. Rama, for instance, is considered the epitome of goodness and the perfect man, even though he repeatedly tormented his wife about chastity. Guess what? After defeating the mighty Ravana, Rama did not receive the celestial award for valor; rather he was forced to atone for his sin. Why? It had nothing to do with his treatment of Sita. Ravana was a Brahmin, and Rama belonged

An effigy of Ravana in flames at the Dussehra festival

to the Kshatriya caste, which is a step below Brahmins. Anyone who kills a Brahmin—intentionally or otherwise—has committed the sin of Brahminicide, which can be absolved only through penance and prayer. Although Rama was an avatar of Vishnu, he received no exemption, and he atoned for his sin by offering prayers to Shiva by creating a *linga* of him at the Ramanathaswamy temple located on the island of Rameswaram in the state of Tamil Nadu.

Ravana was the son of the sage Vaishrava and the demon princess Kaikesi. He inherited most of the good genes of his father yet succumbed to some of the bad ones from his demoness mother—and this eventually led to his downfall. Teeming with virtues, Ravana is described as a devout follower of Shiva, a scholar of the Vedas, a capable ruler, and a veena player par excellence. Such was his proficiency with the veena that in many depictions he is seen holding the instrument. He also was an expert in Hindu astrology and wrote the book *Ravana Samhita*, a treatise on the subject. With astrological information at his fingertips, Ravana timed the birth of his son Meghanada to coincide with an auspicious moment of planetary alignment so that his son would become immortal. Despite Ravana's best efforts, the planet Saturn cast its evil eye on Ravana, thereby nullifying the effect.

Rama and Lakshmana performing Shiva *puja* at Rameswaram after the war

As a great Ayurveda physician, Ravana held a lofty position and wrote seven books on medicine that survive to this day. They originally were written in Sinhala and were later translated to Sanskrit. By this time, you might think Ravana knew animal husbandry and was perhaps a rocket scientist too. Although Ravana is extolled in many regional variations of the Ramayana, he was not known to be the scientific type, nor interested in animal breeding. Yet he remains so popular today that modern Sri Lanka saw a movement to revive Ravana as a cult figure because he was the first person in the island's history to have resisted an alien invader—Rama.

The ten-headed Ravana, the greatest villain of Hinduism

Like Hiranyaksha and Hiranyakashipu before him, Ravana undertook severe austerities to appease Brahma, who granted him immunity from death at the hands of gods, Gandharvas, or demons. Ravana was too conceited to seek immunity from humans, which provided the loophole for Vishnu to dispatch Rama as Ravana's annihilator.

Protected by Brahma's boon, Ravana wasted no time in becoming a dharminator[38] like his predecessors. He stole the palace in Lanka from his stepbrother Kubera. Ravana also appropriated Kubera's flying chariot, Pushpaka, which Ravana later used as a getaway vehicle during his abduction of Sita. He then made good use of the chariot by making aerial attacks on the gods. During one of his conquests Ravana came across Mount Kailash, the abode of Shiva. Unable to steer his flying chariot over the mountain, Ravana attempted to uproot Kailash and relocate it to another part of the world. Shiva woke up from meditation and watched the move with interest. He gently pressed his toe on the mountain, upsetting Ravana's balance. Pinned by the weight of the mountain, Ravana screamed as loudly as he could with his ten heads until Shiva released his toe.

Shiva also coined the name Ravana, which means "the one who screams." Until then Ravana was known as Dashanana. But Ravana was humbled by the experience and was so much in awe of the power of Shiva that Ravana became Shiva's greatest devotee. To placate Shiva, Ravana composed the "Shiva Tandava," a hymn praising his bounty. Shiva, who was known to be easily pleased, was blown away by Ravana's devotion. The Shiva-Ravana association is frequently depicted in temple art where images of Ravana carrying Mount Kailash with Shiva and family at the top can be seen.

Ravana is well known for his knowledge of the Vedas. In fact he is sometimes proclaimed the guru of Rama. On his deathbed Ravana leaned toward Rama and muttered: "Only few more breaths remain in me, but I

---

[38] The Indian author Ashok Banker coined the term *dharminator*, which means "terminator of dharma."

want to share with you this secret. Over the years I have learned that the thing that seduces you will hurt you at the end. And the thing that fails to capture your fancy will become invaluable. I was impatient to abduct Sita and procrastinated about meeting you. It should have been the other way around. I should have spent more time with you as a teacher than an enemy." With these words Ravana breathed his last.

Despite his knowledge of the Vedas, Ravana was a slave to sensual pleasures and a victim of his own ego. His sexual prowess was legendary. It is said that when Hanuman entered Lanka on his mission to find Sita, he found Ravana in bed, surrounded by a bevy of women. We can safely assume they were not listening to his discourse on the Vedas. Ravana had many wives; he even abducted women from neighboring countries, but his principal queen was Mandodari, who loved him sincerely despite his vices and always advised him to follow the path of righteousness. The abduction of Sita was not an exercise in sexual pursuit; rather, he was following his deep desire to conquer the heart of a faithful wife, an effort in which he was sorely defeated.

Before we say farewell again to Jaya and Vijaya—also known as Ravana and Kumbhakarna—let us talk about another popular view of avatars.[39] Many scholars and Shiva devotees view the coming of avatars not as a battle between good and evil but as a tussle between Shiva and Vishnu worshippers. The theory has merit because both Ravana and Mahabali (Bali) were Shiva devotees whom Vishnu annihilated. The theory, however, takes a hit when you realize Parashurama, an avatar of Vishnu's, was himself a Shiva devotee. But, then, Parashurama also suffered a humiliating retreat at the hands of Rama. The same scenario plays out in the case of Hanuman, Rama's trusted sidekick. It is said that Hanuman was actually a manifestation of Shiva himself. But then Hanuman was always in awe of Rama, his lord—which acknowledges Vishnu's supremacy over Shiva.

---

[39] As we discussed earlier, Ravana and Kumbhakarna were originally called Jaya and Vijaya; they were the gatekeepers of Vishnu who were cursed by the Kumaras.

RAVANA—THE GREATEST VILLAIN OF HINDUISM

But for many Shaivites, particularly those from Sri Lanka and Bali (Indonesia), Ravana is a great king on par with Rama. In fact many Tamils believe that they are descendants of Ravana. They so revere Ravana that Tamil regions of Sri Lanka have hardly any Vishnu or Rama temples. In their view North India has always been extending its political and cultural domination of South India by demonizing deities like Ravana and Mahabali. According to the Tamils, the story of Rama as a leader of dharma is a prime example of the Sanskritization and cultural repression of the South.

> *The size of the villain determines the size of the hero. Without Goliath, David is just some punk throwing rocks.*
>
> —BILLY CRYSTAL, 1949–

17

What's in a Name?

After a business visit to Chennai, India, an Australian colleague of mine complained that people in India mispronounced his name calling him, "Naahthen." As a true blue Indian at heart, I felt let down. It's not just Nathan. Many of my colleagues, who head to the subcontinent these days after a change in an outsourcing contract, come back with a standard set of grievances. "Get over it, mate!" I reacted with annoyance. "You have no idea about the plight of people with Indian names living in the West."

What's in a name, you may ask. "A rose by any other name would smell as sweet," right? If you belong to that rarefied set of intellectuals for whom nomenclature holds no charms and who evaluate others according to the quality of their inner selves, my heartiest congratulations on your ideological correctness. You may turn to the next chapter, for the following paragraphs may hold no intellectual stimulation for you. But for mere mortals, for those who have enough red blood in their veins to acknowledge, even to yourselves, that names matter, please continue reading.

Ask me whether names matter, and I would say *plenty* with a capital P. Okay, not all Indians have names like Hiranyakashipu or Kumbhakarna, but many are named after gods or characters from Hindu mythology, and, trust me, they can be hard to remember, let alone pronounce even for those who come from the East. For instance, if you say "Achu," the abridged version of Achuthananda, to an Aussie, I can guarantee the response would be "Whaaaaaaat?" And almost without fail, the next line would be "Is that like a sneeze?" Granted mine is not the garden-variety name, but anything other than John or Chris is not a name for him. And for the next half hour I'll be laboring away to explain my name, its pronunciation, and origin. The coffee has become cold, as I unwittingly make a short tour of Kerala and its culture. Unlike the average American, the typical Aussie should have some familiarity with Indian names. After all, India is not too far from Australia. And once every two years we have a bunch of people, like V. V. S. Laxman, Sachin Tendulkar, and Virat Kohli, who come to Australia for cricket.

Don't get me wrong. I have deep respect for Laxman as a test cricketer—a player at the highest level—but his name has got to be the ultimate name test for a Westerner. His full name is Vangipurappu Venkata Sai Laxman. Surely, a rose by the name VVS Laxman would also smell as sweet as Lincoln Rose. Had Laxman been the name of a Hyderabadi biriyani, I have no doubts that it would be as mouth-watering as any other Andhra cuisine. Yet biriyanis are rarely called Vangipurappu Laxman. You get my point? Having a familiar name is a big advantage in the West. In this age of political correctness, whom do you think a prospective employer will call for an interview: Lalchand Tarachandani or Peter? The truth is, if you go by an Indian name in the West, you're already operating with a handicap. There's nothing much you can do about it other than enjoy the taste. So get used to repeating your name a thousand times at coffee shops, fast food joints, and other places. Unless you become creative and adopt an Aussie name like Sam or Alex to meet your needs temporarily.

Recently another colleague, Paul, came back from a tour of India that had lasted several months. When I saw him chatting with colleagues at work, I dodged and weaved and headed in the opposite direction. I know these conversations. They mostly revolve around mosquitos, dust,

WHAT'S IN A NAME?

humidity, honking on the streets, corruption, and of course poverty. These pampered people are best left to themselves, I thought. Yet I managed to smile as Paul pulled up a chair next to mine in my cubicle.

With bright eyes, he started, "Hi, mate, what an experience! I caught the infamous 'Delhi belly' and was laid down with dysentery for a while, but I enjoyed the whole trip to India, particularly the cuisine and culture." This was a shock to me. What? Am I hearing this right? Finally I had found someone who was not venting their spleen after a trip to India. It is said that India attracts two types of tourists: one who is humbled and enlightened by the experience and another who is bitterly disappointed. Paul seemed to belong in the first category. Paul then went on to wax lyrical about the unique culture of India and the various places he had visited. "Among the states, Kerala was the best, the cleanest," he confessed. Instantly I knew he was speaking the truth. Outside of Kerala, the entire country seems to have been sprayed with *paan*, the betel leaf snack that most Indians use as breath freshener.

There was not a trace of Indian blood in Paul's ancestry, yet he was uttering Indian names and places without any difficulty. "I would've never visited the Jewish synagogue at Kochi, had it not been for your recommendation," he told me and added in a whisper, "I would've never known about Kerala, had it not been for you."

It was a momentous day for me. Forget about my travails with my name. Forget about lost employment opportunities and embarrassment at coffee and pizza joints. They all seem minor now. Having a name that rhymes with a sneeze isn't so bad after all.

Over the years I have learned that names don't matter as much as I once thought. It's just that we are sensitive about other people's lack of familiarity with our names. If names mattered, then Ramakrishna Paramahamsa, Vivekananda, Bhaktivedanta Swami Prabhupada, and Mohandas Gandhi would not have been so respected in the West. If names mattered, then Barack Hussein Obama wouldn't be a phenomenon. It doesn't matter what you are called. What matters is the person inside the name.

RAMA AND THE EARLY AVATARS OF VISHNU

The most irresistible word in the English language has only three letters. And the most powerful of all words is *you*. Whether your name becomes famous, infamous, or completely unknown, it all begins with you.

> *You cannot believe in God until you believe in yourself.*
> —SWAMI VIVEKANANDA, 1863–1902

18

Rama Setu — A Man-made Bridge?

Those days Britain was calling the shots. Back in 1804, when Britain ruled India, a British cartographer observed a narrow strip of land that connects the southern tip of India with Sri Lanka. He marked this long chain of limestone shoals in the calm blue waters of the Indian Ocean as "Adam's Bridge." The mapmaker had no clue that the same bridge was called Rama Setu, or Rama's Bridge, by millions of Indians from time immemorial. This was the bridge their beloved deity Rama used to transport his monkey army to Lanka to apprehend Ravana after he abducted Rama's wife.

At about 50 kilometers long, the bridge consists of a chain of shoals in shallow water that resemble an underwater mountain range. The sea is relatively calm in this area and generates only shallow waves. The water reaches a maximum depth of ten meters, but at some places it's only about one meter deep. Although Sri Lanka is an island, the border between the country and India crosses one of the shoals and constitutes one of the shortest land borders in the world. Temple records say that the bridge was completely above sea level and accessible by foot until 1480 when a cyclone severely damaged the bridge. The bridge is mentioned in the

India's southern neighbor, Sri Lanka

Valmiki Ramayana under the name Setu Bandhana. It is said to have been constructed by Hanuman and the Vanara (monkey) army, whose services Rama enlisted to rescue his wife. Using huge trees, rocks, and boulders, they built a causeway linking the mainland to Lanka.

The bridge is also cited in other, later works. Ibn Khordadbeh, a ninth-century Persian geographer, calls it Set Bandhai, or Bridge of the Sea, in his *Book of Roads and Kingdoms*. A Dutch cartographer in 1747 marked the bridge as Ramancoil, or Rama's Temple, probably an association with the temple at Rameswaram Island.[40] The name Adam's Bridge was probably inspired by a legend in Gnostic sources that later appeared in Islamic texts. As the story goes, when Adam was expelled from Paradise, he crossed the bridge to reach Adam's Peak in Sri Lanka. Adam is believed

---

[40] The bridge starts from Rameswaram Island, an Indian island off the tip of India that lies between the mainland and Sri Lanka. Rameswaram Island, the site of the famous Ramanathaswamy Temple, is also known as Pamban Island.

RAMA SETU–A MAN-MADE BRIDGE?

to have stood repentant on one foot for one thousand years, leaving a large hollow mark resembling a footprint near the summit.[41]

Regardless of its historical significance, the bridge proved to be a blessing for the coastlines of both countries by acting as a protective barrier against storms and tsunamis. The bridge is credited with protecting the coastal line of Kerala in the devastating 2004 Indian Ocean tsunami. Yet sometimes the bridge is also seen as an impediment to navigation because trade between India and Sri Lanka is conducted on small boats and dinghies. Larger ocean-going vessels from the West have to navigate around Sri Lanka to reach India's east coast instead taking the shorter route through the Palk Strait, where the bridge is located (see map). In 2005 the Indian government approved a multimillion-dollar project to create a shipping channel by dredging through Rama's bridge. The channel was expected to shorten the trip past Sri Lanka by about 400 kilometers. But the project got bogged down in debate and controversy. Concerns

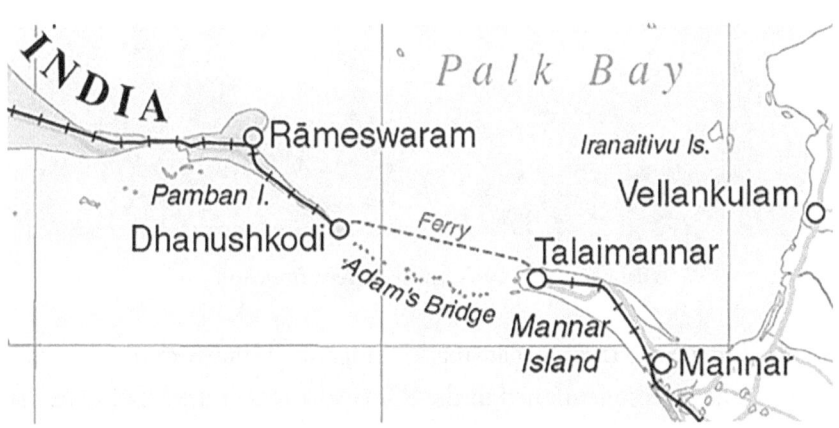

Rama's Bridge and the surrounding areas, derived from United Nations map

---

[41] Adam's Peak is a tall conical mountain located in central Sri Lanka. A rock formation near the summit looks strangely like footprints. Sri Lankan Buddhists believe the footprints are Buddha's, Hindus regard them as Shiva's, and Christians and Muslims believe them to be those of Adam or Saint Thomas.

included potential loss of thorium deposits[42] in the area, increased risk of damage from storms and tsunamis, and the impact on the area's ecology and wealth. However, the key reason to nix the project was that it would destroy the remnants of an ancient monument and a sacred heritage of millions of Hindus. "The bridge is as holy to Hindus as the Wailing Wall is to the Jews, the Vatican to Catholics, Bodh Gaya to Buddhists, and Mecca to Muslims," claimed the president of a US lobbying group.

Aerial photo of Adam's Bridge, as seen from Sri Lanka

Is Rama Setu truly a man-made bridge, as Hindus claim? No one knows. The places mentioned in the Ramayana match the location of the bridge. According to Hindu tradition, Rama lived during the Treta Yuga, a period of time that began more than two million years ago. Although this

---

[42] The coastal sands south of Rama Setu are believed to contain 32 percent of the known thorium reserves in the world. Thorium is valued as a future nuclear fuel and a cleaner alternative to uranium.

claim may seem absurd on the surface, the Ramayana has a historical charm, even though the epic is replete with characters that are not human beings. For instance, Hanuman and Sugriva are talking monkeys, while the king of Lanka is a ten-headed demon. The scientific types do not buy this argument and point out that the Ramayana also describes flying chariots and Hanuman transporting a massive mountain. In prestigious scientific journals they expound on their theories about the geological process that gave rise to the structure, such as down warping, mantle plume activity, longshore drifting, and block faulting. US satellite footage from 2002, however, shows the formation to be a long broken bridge beneath the ocean's surface, although the origin and age of these structures could not be determined

The presence of a loose layer of sand beneath the corals for an entire stretch convinced S. Badrinarayanan, the former director of the Geological Survey of India, to claim that Rama Setu is not a natural formation. According to him, "Coral reefs are formed only on hard surfaces. During our study we found that the formation at Adam's Bridge is nothing but boulders of coral reefs. When we drilled for investigation, we found that there was loose sand two or three meters below the reefs. Such a natural formation is impossible. Unless somebody has transported them and dumped them there, those reefs could not have come [from] there." But the Archeological Survey of India issued a report stating that it had found no evidence that the bridge was anything but natural. A 2007 publication of India's National Remote Sensing Agency, however, says the structure may be man-made.

In short, for every study and survey that says the bridge is man-made, there's another one that says it is not. Whether the bridge is a natural structure or an engineering masterpiece, we may never know. But there's little doubt about its historical significance. It's only fitting that a bridge used by Rama and later by Adam be declared a World Heritage Site and protected from destruction by humans.

19

The Doggedness of Agni Pariksha

Not too long ago, in the Indian state of Gujarat, a rape survivor was asked to undergo a "purity test" by balancing a 40-kilogram stone on her head before she could live with her husband again. Practiced in certain areas of rural India, the test is part of a cultural tradition that requires women whose virtue has been tainted by sexual abuse or whose chastity is under question to prove their purity by undertaking a physically arduous task. The test had its origin in the Ramayana where Rama, after rescuing his wife, doubts her chastity while in captivity. Because of his doubts, he arranges an Agni Pariksha, or trial by fire. In the epic Sita walks into the blazing pyre and miraculously emerges unharmed by the flames, confirming her purity. The fire god Agni, represented by the blazing fire, is believed to destroy anything impure and sinful.

Ancient India celebrated chastity. A woman who had conquered her primal urges was considered the foundation of human society. It was also believed that chastity bestowed women with special powers that they could use to protect themselves from all harm. Such was the power of Sita's chastity that the burning flames did not even singe her hair. And

The Agni Pariksha of Sita (unknown artist, ca. 1900)

Sita was not the only woman with such powers. Sacred Hindu lore is full of tales of chaste woman with magical powers. One was Damayanti, the wife of King Nala. The king gambled away his kingdom in a game of dice. Penniless, he was forced to leave his city and seek shelter in the forest. Like a dutiful wife, Damayanti shared her husband's misfortune by accompanying him into the forest. There Nala became worried about the safety of his wife. He ran away from her, hoping she would go back to her father's house and leave the dangers of forest behind. Damayanti lost her way in the forest and was about to be swallowed by a python when a hunter came to her rescue. Later the hunter attempted to force himself on her, but the strength of her chastity caused him to implode in flames.

THE DOGGEDNESS OF AGNI PARIKSHA

Stories like these emphasized the allure of chastity. They also fostered a notion that women fell prey to rape only when they were insufficiently chaste. The onus was on the victim of rape to prove her innocence, by undertaking the Agni Pariksha. If fire did not harm her, she was considered pure. The trial by fire was, however, not infallible, as another story attests. A Brahmin learned that his wife had been unfaithful to him, but she lied and pleaded innocence. He commanded her to undergo a trial by fire. The disloyal wife stepped into the pit of fire and emerged unharmed. When the Brahmin demanded an explanation from Agni, the fire god told him that the place where his wife had liaisons with other men was a holy spot, so sins committed there are purified. For the same reason the people of Ayodhya did not believe Sita's trial by fire guaranteed her chastity and demanded a second test.

Incidentally, the demand for an additional chastity test was not in the Valmiki Ramayana but was appended to the original version years later in a chapter entitled "Uttara Kanda." Many scholars believe that the story of Rama and Sita ended with Sita's passing the fire test and the couple's living happily ever after in the kingdom of Ayodhya. The "Uttara Kanda," the last chapter in the Valmiki version, extends the ending by including Sita's exile based on gossip by a *dhobi* and the additional test of chastity. Another story that is believed to have been added to the Valmiki version was Rama's killing of Shambuka for violating his caste dharma.

The most important addition to the Ramayana, however, was the motif of Maya Sita. Absent in the Valmiki Ramayana, the idea of Maya Sita first appeared in the Kurma Purana and became a recurring theme in later versions of the Ramayana. In this version, Agni creates an exact double of Sita called Maya Sita and swaps her for the real Sita at the time of her abduction. The Maya Sita is flown to Lanka and held captive by Ravana, while the real Sita is protected in Agni's refuge. After Rama defeats Ravana and returns to Ayodhya, the Agni Pariksha becomes the device through which the real Sita and Maya Sita trade places. While the real Sita emerges from the fire ordeal, Maya Sita perishes in the flames. Clearly, the later versions of the Ramayana went to extraordinary lengths to protect the image of a perfect Rama. Devotees could not bear Sita being kidnapped by the demon Ravana and defiled by his touch since chaste women are automatically protected by divine intervention. The Maya Sita motif saved Sita from falling prey to the vices of Ravana and protected her purity.

The Maya Sita motif reaffirmed the belief that chaste women possess such magical powers that even gods themselves manifest on Earth to protect their chastity. While the Maya Sita helped Sita preserve her purity, it did not provide any relief for ordinary Indian women faced with increasing sexual violence. On the contrary, the burden on women to prove their chastity became entrenched in society. Sometimes it is said that the Agni Pariksha in the Ramayana legitimized women's oppression in India.

Although India has made steady progress in improving the status of women—including having a woman prime minster well before several advanced countries of the world—retrograde views about women are rampant in some quarters of Indian society. In modern India sexual violence has been a serious and widespread problem, and perpetrators often go unpunished. The brutal rape of Jyoti Singh, a 23-year-old college student, in 2012 sparked nationwide discussion of violence against woman. Her death came to symbolize women's struggle to end the rape culture and the tradition of blaming the victim rather than the perpetrator. In response the government of India has introduced a series of measures to prioritize crimes against women, such as the setting up of fast-track courts and criminalizing stalking. Laws were swiftly enacted, but attitudes and mentalities take generations to change, as India is slowly finding out.

> *Every woman should be able to go about the day—to walk the street, or ride the bus—and be safe and be treated with the respect and dignity that she deserves.*
>
> —BARACK OBAMA, 1961–

❋ ❋ ❋

20

The Ramayana of Valmiki

If Rama is a beloved deity of India and regarded as a historical figure, praise goes to the sage and poet Valmiki, who brought life and color to this character in his monumental work, the Ramayana. Over the years many versions of the story of Rama have come and gone, yet the earliest one by Valmiki—known as the Valmiki Ramayana—is still considered the most prestigious, authoritative, and influential version. So was Valmiki a literary genius of incomparable talent? Well, not much is known about Valmiki other than that he lived sometime between 500 BCE and 200 CE. Legends about the early life of Valmiki, however, cast him in an entirely different light. He is believed to have born into a family of robbers, and his original name was Ratnakar.

As the legend goes, Ratnakar was a devoted family man and a hunter by profession. To make ends meet he sometimes robbed travelers in the forest. One day he came across the Saptarishis (seven sages), who admonished him about his behavior and warned him that he alone was responsible for his actions, or karma.[43] The sages' words had a profound impact on Ratnakar. That evening he asked his wife whether she would

---

[43] Another version of the same story mentions the sage Narada instead of the Saptarishis.

share the consequences of his sins. She replied that one enjoys the fruits of one's own actions, and these cannot be shared with anybody. Ratnakar became despondent. When he met the Saptarishis again, they told him to chant the name of Rama—which should absolve him of his sins. Because of his low birth Ratnakar was adjudged unqualified to chant Rama's name directly. Instead, the sages taught him the mantra *"mara mara."* It is said that Ratnakar diligently repeated the mantra for such a long time that his body became covered with termites. Finally the Saptarishis called on Ratnakar to come out of *tapas*. Because Ratnakar had been living in a termite's nest, he was called Valmiki, or "one born out of a termite nest." Little did the Saptarishis know that they had transformed a part-time robber into an immortal literary genius, for when Ratnakar uttered the mantra repeatedly, the syllables blended into *"(ma)rama rama(ra),"* thereby accruing the meritorious karmic fruits of chanting Rama's name.

Did Valmiki compose the Ramayana? It is plausible that the Ramayana existed even before the time of Valmiki, for the Ramayana belongs to the genre of Hindu texts called *smriti,* or remembered. The *smriti* texts were believed to be the recollection of historical events by well-known authorities. In those times, the story was transmitted orally, for writing came much later. It is likely subsequent storytellers added their own embellishments during oral transmission. Valmiki perhaps was at the end of a long chain of oral transmitters and simply retold the Ramayana in the form of a beautiful composition. Today Valmiki's Ramayana is clearly the oldest surviving version.

The Valmiki Ramayana has about 25,000 verses presented in seven sections, or *kandas*. It is written in the language Sanskrit, which holds a lofty place in ancient Hindu traditions not only as a sacred language but as the most suitable language for praising deities. That is why the Valmiki Ramayana commands more authority and respect than all other renditions of the story. For that reason Valmiki is celebrated as the first poet and the Valmiki Ramayana as the first Hindu epic poem.

There is an interesting story of how Valmiki got the inspiration to write the first verse. One day he was going to the river for a bath when he saw a hunter shoot down a Krauncha[44] bird that was mating. It was one of a pair, and the surviving bird flew around in agony. This tragic scene inspired Valmiki to write the first verse and originated from Valmiki's sorrow about the separation of lovers.

In the Ramayana, Valmiki himself plays a small role, appearing at different times—in the "Bala Kanda" and the "Uttara Kanda." For instance, Rama is seen visiting Valmiki's ashram during Rama's exile to the forest. Later in the story Valmiki provides shelter to Sita in his hermitage when Rama banishes her to the forest. Her twin sons, Lava and Kusha, were born at the hermitage. Valmiki provides the education and training in military skills for the boys. Later, when Rama performs the Ashvamedha sacrifice, he learns about his wife and children and ultimately reunites with his family—at the intervention of Valmiki.

Valmiki trains Lava and Kusha in archery (artist unknown)

---

[44] Krauncha bird is the crane.

The Ramayana of Valmiki affirms the values of the social order of the day. Valmiki portrays Rama not as a supernatural being but as a human with limitations. Throughout the epic Rama encounters many moral dilemmas. Upon his exile to the forest, why did Rama take Sita and Lakshmana along with him? Was Shurpanakha's disfigurement necessary? Why did Rama use unfair means to kill Vali? Why did Rama make Sita undergo tests of purity, not once but twice? Why did he unfairly kill Shambuka? In the Ramayana, Rama overcomes these moral dilemmas by simply adhering to dharma. The emphasis, in those days, was on performing one's dharma without fail, whether it meant honoring a spouse, parent, brother, or relative. The Valmiki Ramayana urges deference to dharma even at great social or personal cost. The text thus became a favorite of rulers (Kshatriyas) and priest (Brahmins), especially those among the upper castes.

Not all Sanskrit versions of the Ramayana accept Valmiki's view of dharma or societal rules. It is said that discontent with Rama's decisions led to the composition of alternative versions of the Ramayana. In Bhavabhuti's eighth-century Sanskrit play *Uttararamacharita*, for instance, Rama blames himself for his cruelty to Sita. He also rues having executed Shambuka because as a king he was duty bound to uphold the social order of the day. Despite the ideological differences in the latter-day texts, the Valmiki Ramayana is by far the most influential telling of the Ramayana in Sanskrit.

> *Either write something worth reading or do something worth writing.*
> —BENJAMIN FRANKLIN, 1706-1790

21

A Mosque and Temple Controversy

King Rama is believed to have lived around 3000 BCE, but if you were to judge the popularity of Rama today on a scale of one to ten, what score do you think he would merit? A nine or perhaps even a ten? Back in 1987, Doordarshan, Indian's public broadcaster, gave Rama an internal rating of three. That was when a proposal to air the Ramayana in 78 episodes for television was presented to Doordarshan. The broadcaster balked, saying people in a secular country had no time or interest to watch religious serials. However, yielding to political pressure, Doordarshan began telecasting the show. The broadcaster's executives soon realized how badly they had misjudged the public interest in such a show. The serial not only created a TV revolution but held the record as India's most-watched television program of all time.[45]

The Ramayana fever spread through the nation like an Indian monsoon at the end of summer. During the daily broadcasts of the episodes,

---

[45] Although the Ramayana had the highest ratings at that time, telecast of the epic Mahabharata later garnered even more viewers.

the nation came to a complete stop—with deserted streets and empty public transport. The fever reached a crescendo five years later when Rama became embroiled in the one of the biggest controversies of modern India. In December 1992 Hindu activists shocked the nation when they demolished a 16th-century mosque called Babri Masjid in the state of Uttar Pradesh. It was supposedly a tit for tat—almost 500 years earlier Muslims had demolished a Hindu monument of Rama there to make way for their mosque. The 1992 mosque demolition set off clashes between Hindus and Muslims all over India and led to the deaths of about two thousand people.

Two years later the Supreme Court justice Bharucha confidently predicted that the controversy was "a storm that will pass." Yet even several decades after the demolition of the disputed shrine, the storm has refused to subside. The political party representing the prime minister, Narendra Modi, said in its 2014 general election manifesto that it would explore all possibilities within the framework of the constitution to facilitate the construction of a Ram temple at the disputed site.

Why are Hindus intent on building a temple in the place of the mosque? The root of the conflict goes back to several hundred years in history. The Babri Mosque was built in 1528 CE, two years after Baber, the founder of Muslim Mughal empire, invaded India. Not only was the mosque built in Rama's birthplace of Ayodhya, an existing Hindu monument in the same location was razed to make way for the mosque. Should that be sufficient grounds to demolish the mosque and rebuild the Rama temple? Certainly not, in almost all cases; however, the circumstances are unique to this controversy because substantial evidence exists of an unbroken tradition of worship by Hindus at this site—both before and after the construction of the mosque.

Historically, Ayodhya is a significant city and one of India's seven sacred cities. In addition to being Rama's birthplace, Ayodhya was the capital of Rama's kingdom and that of his father before him. Babri Masjid was built on a hill known as Ramkot, which means "Rama's fort." Hindus claim that, to build the mosque, the Mughals destroyed a structure that marked the birthplace of Rama. The Muslims denied they did any such thing. In

A MOSQUE AND TEMPLE CONTROVERSY

Babri Masjid before its destruction in 1992

1767, about 250 years after the mosque was built, an Austrian priest visiting the site recorded that many Hindu pilgrims came to the site to worship at a small platform that marked the birthplace of Rama. This platform stood next to the Babri Mosque. According to the priest, it was common knowledge among the people of Ayodhya that the Muslims had forcibly taken over the site for their mosque. An inscription in Babri Masjid said the mosque was built in 1528 by Mir Baqi, who was Bābur's general. However, this information does not appear in *Bāburnāma*, the memoir left by Bābur, because the pages surrounding the event are mysteriously missing.

The British annexed Ayodhya (then known as Oudh) in 1856, marking the end of Muslim rule in the region. Immediately thereafter, some Hindu ascetics claimed ownership of the site since, they said, the mosque was forcibly built on Rama's birthplace. After due consideration the British decided that Hindus could perform *puja* at the platform as the birthplace of Rama. This practice continued without incident until 1949, two years after India declared its independence. Under the cover of darkness, Hindu activists broke into the mosque and placed in it statues of Rama Lalla, the infant form of Rama. This incident was escalated and brought to the attention of Jawaharlal Nehru, who was then prime minister of India. Three days later the central government ordered the removal of the idols with immediate effect, but the district magistrate did not execute the order, fearing riots and backlash. Meanwhile, throngs of devotees, numbering in the thousands, came from far to offer their prayers to Rama. This did not give rise to much protest from the Muslims living in the area because the mosque was in disuse since 1936.

Three months later the Hindu Mahasabha, a nationalistic movement that believes Hindustan[46] is the land of Hindus, issued a flier marking not only the birthday of Rama but also his birthplace. The flier also claimed that the mosque was standing atop fourteen original pillars of a Hindu temple that had been demolished by the Mughals. A local court issued a restraining order to prevent anyone from removing the statues and interfering with the *puja*.

Muslim worshippers praying at Babri Masjid after destruction

---

[46] Hindustan refers to the modern day Republic of India. Historically the term referred to the Indian subcontinent and included countries like India, Pakistan, Bangladesh, etc. Sometimes Afghanistan was also included in the list.

A MOSQUE AND TEMPLE CONTROVERSY

By 1988 the Ramayana TV serial had become a national sensation of India, a country where Hindus constitute 82 percent of the population. Four years later, in December 1992, after the conclusion of a political rally, a larger number of Hindu activists climbed on top of the mosque with the help of ropes. They brought along iron rods, which they used to dismantle the domes, including the large main dome, and then cleaned up the debris. The statues of Rama had been removed from the site beforehand. The activists then erected a small temple on the site and placed the statues in it. Throughout, police stationed at the site did nothing, and the central police force withdrew from the site.

The razing of the mosque triggered nationwide protests and rioting between Hindus and Muslims in which so many died. Hindu nationalism was about preserving the heritage of India, but this act went against the age-old Hindu tradition of showing tolerance and religious maturity. Although many believe Bābur was an insensitive ruler, most Hindus condemned the razing of the mosque.

Historically, this was not the first time a religious structure, albeit in disuse, was razed. Many writings, both Indian and non-Indian, report that at least 3,000 Hindu temples in North and South India were destroyed by Muslim rulers over the centuries, including Muhammad of Ghazni, Bābur, Aurangzeb, and the overzealous sultans of Bijapur. Many of the temples were not just destroyed but converted to mosques. The Somnath Temple in Gujarat, for instance, was destroyed at least 17 times by Islamic rulers and rebuilt as many times by Hindu kings. After India's independence, Hindu activists repeatedly said they would stop demanding the restoration of other temple sites if Muslims, in a cooperative spirit as fellow citizens, agreed to surrender three sites most sacred to Hindus. These include the Gyanavapi mosque in Varanasi, the Babri Masjid in Ayodhya, and the Shahi Idgah Mosque at Mathura. Needless to say, no concessions were forthcoming from Muslim leaders of that time.

In 2003, under the orders of an Indian court, the Archaeological Survey of India, the premiere organization for the protection of cultural heritage, published its investigation report that confirmed the existence of a 10th-century Hindu temple under the Babri Masjid. And in 2010, in a landmark ruling, the Allahabad High Court, the supreme court of the state of Uttar Pradesh, ruled the disputed land was to be divided into three equal parts: one-third for the construction of a Rama temple, one-third would go to the board of trustees representing Babri Masjid, and the remaining third to a Hindu denomination. Control of the main disputed section, where the mosque had been located, went to the Hindus. However, both the Hindu and Muslim organizations appealed, arguing the site should not be divided, and the Supreme Court of India promptly suspended the lower court's order. After many proposals and failed efforts to reach a settlement, the Supreme Court in 2017 called for an amicable settlement, saying the sensitive and sentimental issue is best settled out of court.

As of this writing, the controversy has not ended. But its ramifications are clear: demolition of Babri Masjid has significantly challenged the delicate institution of pluralism and secularism carefully built into India's constitution.

> *The ultimate measure of a man is not where he stands in moments of comfort and convenience, but where he stands at times of challenge and controversy.*
> —MARTIN LUTHER KING, JR, 1929–1968

22

Hanuman – The Ideal Devotee

Of all the songs that invoke the glory of Rama, one of my favorites is the Carnatic song, "Rama Nannu Brovara." Composed by the 18th-century poet-saint Tyagaraja—whom we briefly mentioned in book 2—the song cries out to the lord, pleading, "O Rama, please protect me!" A passionate devotee of Rama's, Tyagaraja believed in the notion that divinity can be attained through devotion plus a good dash of music.[47] According to him, Rama was the perfect god, and humans should emulate him. But what if you can't be Rama? The next best thing is to become a Rama devotee and seek his protection.

And that advice has been taken by many: poets, saints, and even ordinary people. Rama has had many devotees from afar and abroad, yet the greatest of them was Hanuman, the monkey god. The monkey commander was a dutiful Sherpa to Rama, guiding him in the mighty battle against Ravana. Hanuman's loyalty to Rama is proverbial, and he's considered the epitome of simplicity and faithfulness. Hanuman displayed

---

[47] The philosophy of Indian classical music is rooted in the concept of *Nada Brahma*—which means the whole universe was created from sound, and only sound existed in the very beginning.

exceptional simian capabilities by leaping from India to Sri Lanka as part of a reconnaissance mission for the invaders but was captured by the rakshasas, who greased his tail and set it on fire. With a burning tail, he destroyed their capital city. Back in India, he uprooted trees and carried huge boulders from the Himalayas to build the famous Rama Setu bridge, which allowed Rama's army to cross the straits. When Lakshmana was fatally wounded in battle, Hanuman flew to the Himalayas and brought back medicinal herbs that revived Lakshmana.

What distinguished Hanuman from other gods is the way he achieved his divine status—through his deep-seated dedication to Rama. When Rama returned to Ayodhya after defeating Ravana, he asked Hanuman to choose a reward for his great service. The faithful monkey asked only for permission to live as long as the story of Rama can be told to the world. Thus Hanuman became a *chiranjeevi*, joining the elite company of Mahabali, Parashurama, and other distinguished immortals of Hinduism.

Hanuman, the monkey god and Rama's greatest devotee

Many versions of Hanuman's birth exist in mythology, but almost all say Anjana was his mother. Originally an *apsara*, Anjana was transformed into a monkey because of a curse. In one version Anjana was worshipping Shiva when King Dasharatha performed a horse sacrifice and received the divine pudding for begetting children. Although the king distributed the pudding among his queens—which led to the birth of his illustrious sons Rama, Lakshmana, Bharata, and Shatrughna—a portion of the pudding was snatched by a kite that flew off with it but dropped it over a forest. The wind god Vayu guided the falling pudding with laser precision into the outstretched hands of Anjana, who consumed it and gave birth to Hanuman.

In another version of the story, Shiva and Parvati transform themselves into monkeys and engage in monkey *maithuna* and conceive a child. Shiva realizes that the child will be a monkey and asks Vayu to place the gestating seed in the womb of Anjana. While Anjana was looking for fruit to eat, Vayu appears as breeze, lifts her garments up to her waist, and places the seed in her womb. Another version of Hanuman's birth states that he was the son of Shiva and Mohini, the female form of Vishnu. The kinetic energy of their courtship was converted to potential energy and stored in sacred form. When Anjana and her husband, Kesari, a Vanara[48] and monkey chieftain, prayed to Shiva for a son, Shiva asked Vayu to place the energy inside Anjana's womb. A variation of the same myth associates the union of Shiva and Mohini with the origin of Swami Ayyappan, a popular god of Kerala.

Hanuman might be an ordinary monkey to you and me, but he was called Sundar, the beautiful, by his mother, as described in the fifth book of the Ramayana, "Sundara Kanda." Shortly after his birth, the beautiful one latched onto his mother's breast and suckled until she had no milk left. Still hungry, the baby saw the rising sun and mistook it for a piece of fruit. He leaped into the sky to devour it. When Indra, the ruler of the heavens, saw an unidentified object darting toward the heavens, he hurled his thunderbolt at it. The thunderbolt intercepted Hanuman and the impact made him fall on a rock. But the fall also shattered his jaw (*hanu*), thus inspiring the name Hanuman. Vayu became uncontrollably irate upon seeing his son lying unconscious. He used his power, as god of the wind, to withdraw air from the universe. The gods in the heavens experienced breathing difficulty and nausea. Indra realized his folly and groveled at Vayu's feet. To appease Vayu, Hanuman was bestowed with superhuman powers.

Many tales relate the astounding feats of Hanuman. In some, imagination seems to be running amok for great liberties have been taken

---

[48] The term *Vanara* means forest dweller, but it is often used as a synonym for monkey.

with poetic license. For instance, in the battle of Lanka, Lakshmana was wounded in several places and only the leaves of the herb Sanjeevani could restore him to health. Hanuman was urgently dispatched to fetch the herb. Ravana was equally determined to prevent him from getting it. He sent the demon Kalanemi to stop Hanuman on his way, and Ravana promised half his kingdom as reward. Disguised as a sage, Kalanemi erected a hermitage near a lake in the Himalayas to trap Hanuman. While Hanuman was passing the hermitage, he asked the sage's permission to quench his thirst—which the sage cheerfully agreed. When Hanuman entered the lake, Kalanemi unleashed a crocodile that grabbed Hanuman's feet with its powerful jaws. But the crocodile proved no match for Hanuman. Surprisingly the crocodile transformed into an *apsara* at death and thanked Hanuman for releasing her from a curse. In gratitude the *apsara* revealed to Hanuman that the ascetic was Kalanemi in disguise, whereupon Hanuman caught the phony sage by the leg and whirled him through the air to Lanka, where he fell before Ravana and his ministers.

With Kalanemi disposed of, Hanuman started looking for the herb, but he couldn't locate it. But Lakshmana was nearing death, so Hanuman grabbed the entire mountain and flew with it to Lanka. As he was passing Ayodhya, Bharata mistakenly thought the cyclone created by Hanuman's course was the work of some demon. He shot an arrow at Hanuman and brought him down. Aggrieved at his mistake, Bharata apologized to Hanuman. To make amends Bharata offered to transport Hanuman to Lanka with another arrow. But Hanuman declined the offer and flew with his own strength. As he was approaching Lanka, he noticed that the moon was about to rise. The herb was known to be effective only before moonrise. So Hanuman swallowed the moon to preserve the herb's efficacy and dashed to Lanka and revived the wounded hero.

We can only assume that Hanuman was able to disgorge the moon after Lakshmana was healed. Incidentally, Hanuman is one of the few gods who is present for both the Rama and Krishna incarnations of Vishnu. While the tale about getting the herb for Lakshmana is from the Ramayana, the Mahabharata provides an interesting account of a meeting between Hanuman and his half-brother Bhima, who was the son of Vayu and Kunti. It happened during the Pandavas' exile. The Pandavas, the five sons of Pandu and Kunti, were traveling through a forest when the sweet scent of Saugandhika (white ginger lily) wafted through the air. Charmed by its fragrance, Draupadi, the common wife of the Pandavas, wanted to possess the flower and asked Bhima to find some. As he went looking for the celestial flower, the hulking Bhima destroyed plants and trees in his way until he tripped over the tail of an old monkey that was resting in his path. Annoyed, Bhima ordered the monkey to move out of his way. The monkey sought Bhima's help to move its tail, for the animal had grown old and weak. Always proud of his strength, Bhima tried to lift the tail, but the appendage began to grow. Unable to raise the tail with his arms, Bhima attempted to lift it with his club, but it broke in the attempt. A frustrated Bhima looked closely at the monkey and realized that it was his half-brother Hanuman. This episode highlighted the difference between the brothers. While Hanuman was always humble, Bhima was proud of his power and strength.

Hanuman was not just humble but simple-hearted too. Once Hanuman observed Sita wearing *sindoor* (a red cosmetic powder) along the parting of her hair. When Hanuman asked Sita about it, she told him that vermillion was symbolic of a married woman and signifies a happy married life. According to her, a woman seeking longevity for her husband uses the red powder throughout her life. Hanuman mulled over Sita's response and reasoned that if a pinch of vermillion can ensure a long life for the master, then applying it to his entire body would make him immortal. That day he applied vermillion all over his body and went to the court. Everyone burst out laughing except Rama, who realized how much Hanuman was obsessed with devotion to his master.

Hanuman is known by other names, including Anjaneya (son of Anjana), Vayuputra (son of Vayu), Maruti, and Bajrang Bali (the strong one.) The ruler of the Vanara kingdom, Sugriva, does not have any temples dedicated to him, but Hanuman temples are found everywhere, not only in India but in other countries. A 85-foot statue of Hanuman,

The 85-foot statue of Hanuman in Trinidad

installed in 2003 and known as *Karya Siddhi Hanuman*, is the pride of the small village of Carapichaima in central Trinidad. But that's not the tallest Hanuman statue. Paritala, in Andhra Pradesh, hosts a 135-foot statue of Hanuman.

In temples where Hanuman is the chief deity, he is usually coated with vermillion. Hanuman is also found in temples dedicated to Rama,

HANUMAN-THE IDEAL DEVOTEE

where the monkey god is shown kneeling on one side or standing behind Rama. Like Ganesha, Hanuman was a lifelong bachelor.[49] Devotees pray to Hanuman daily by reading the "Hanuman Chalisa," a devotional song composed by the poet Tulsidas. Hanuman is highly revered in India, so stray monkeys in India get a free pass from mischief because of their association with Hanuman.

The greatest tributes to Hanuman appear in "Sundara Kanda," the only chapter of the Ramayana in which the hero is not Rama but Hanuman. His selflessness, strength, and devotion to Rama are emphasized in beautiful, rhythmic descriptions meant to be read aloud. In a 2016 interview US President Barack Obama revealed before his final State of the Union address that a statuette of Hanuman is among the few items he carries in his pocket, and he seeks inspiration from it whenever he feels tired or discouraged.

---

[49] While steadfastly chaste in the Sanskrit tradition, Hanuman has wives and children in non-Indian versions of the Ramayana, such as the Thai *Ramakien*.

23

Hanuman — A Monkey or Ape?

Whether Hanuman is a monkey or an ape is an intriguing question that appears to have no definitive answer. In the Ramayana Hanuman manifests as a human in his ability to communicate as well as comprehend things. A member of the sect of civilized Vanaras, he is able to mingle with humans and is renowned for his knowledge of the Vedas. All these abilities lead us to believe he is an ape, a mammal closer to humans in the evolutionary tree. Yet physical appearance tells a different story. Although the contours of his face are characteristically simian, Hanuman is often described as the possessor of a long tail, which he used not only to set fire to Lanka upon his capture but also to humiliate his half-brother Bhima for his pride. Unlike most monkeys, apes do not possess tails. Thus Hanuman is in the category of monkeys or, more precisely, tailed monkeys.

In Hindu mythology, Hanuman is said to be a Vanara. Although scholars have associated Vanaras with humanoids or tribal people using totems, the word *Vanara* means forest dwelling. It has come to mean a monkey, even though the association is not clearly established. Brahma is said to have created the Vanaras to help Rama in his duel with Ravana. On Brahma's orders the gods began to sire progeny that resembled monkeys, who then organized into armies and spread through forests.

It is well known that simians dread water. Some have even drowned in the moats that zoos often use to confine them. When they find themselves out of their depth in water, monkeys usually flounder around in a flurry of limbs. Their fear of water is described in the Ramayana in an episode in which Sugriva, the monkey king, divides his army into four

The monkey god Hanuman holding a mace and carrying the mountain

divisions and sends them to look for Sita in each of the four directions. Hanuman was specifically chosen to lead the southern division since the evidence at hand suggested that Ravana might have gone south with Sita. Hanuman and his monkey comrades searched through forest until they reached the ocean. Alarmed at the sight of water, they did not know what to do and sat dejected near the seashore. There they encountered Sampati, a vulture and brother of Jatayu, the vulture king. The bird told them about Lanka, its fortifications and its distance from the sea. Hanuman, drawing strength from his meditation, began to increase in size. Roaring like thunder, Hanuman took off vertically like a Lockheed Martin F-22 Raptor fighter aircraft and hurtled through the skies to Lanka. Later in the epic, at Rama's request, Hanuman and his Vanara army construct the Rama Setu, the bridge that connects the southern tip of India to Sri Lanka and allowed the simians to stay clear of water.

Whether Hanuman is just an ordinary monkey with supernatural powers or a member of a species as advanced as humans, we'll never know. What we know is Hanuman has helped monkeys survive in India, and they enjoy a measure of respect and veneration because of their association with the monkey god. In modern times the monkey population has been on the rise, with an increasing number moving into cities, thanks to urban sprawl and deforestation. Many have seamlessly adapted to the new environment and have been found stealing food, picking pockets, and even drinking alcohol. The monkey population is thriving, but other animals, such as Bengal tigers, Indian lions, snow leopards, and one-horned rhinos, have either entered the endangered list or are struggling to survive in their motherland.

24

Sankat Mochan Hanuman

The bad news kept flowing. Your company has just announced that "to accelerate the transformation for the future," it is closing the local plant and laying off 1,500 workers—including you. Lately things haven't been going too well. A few weeks back, your mother was diagnosed with lung cancer, and doctors say she has only months to live. And recently your son missed out on admission to the local university, although it had seemed almost guaranteed. According to the vice chancellor, applications were more competitive this year than previously. "Gosh, why is the world against me?" Your nerves are on edge as you anxiously await the next piece of bad news. The pendulum of your life has swung wildly out of control and your soul cries out for peace. In Hindu astrology you are going through that dreaded astrological phase in life known as Sade Sati, a seven-and-half-year period of extraordinary difficulties while the deity Shani traverses your zodiac sign. Who is Shani and why does he make everyone's life miserable?

Shani is the astrological personification of the planet Saturn and one of the nine planetary deities collectively known as Navagraha, which includes gods like Surya, Chandra, Shani, and others. All have powerful gazes, and several are considered malevolent. The most frightful among them is undoubtedly Shani, whose glance decapitated Shiva's son. (We'll get to that story shortly.) Shani is known to routinely cast an evil eye, and his destructive impact is felt during Sade Sati in particular. How can you minimize the effect of Shani? Vedic astrology says the destiny of a person is determined by the planetary position at the time of birth. An unfortunate soul born under the influence of Shani is doomed—unless the person is a devotee of Hanuman.

In mythology Shani is the son of sun god Surya and surrogate Chhaya. If you recall, the sun god's wife Sanjna left her husband leaving a handmaiden, Chhaya, in her place as she could not bear his intense brightness.[50] The name Shani literally means the "slow-moving one." Shani is physically slow and walks with a conspicuous limp because of an injured knee—courtesy of a childhood fight with his stepbrother Yama. Shani is the farthest from Earth of the visible planets and takes about 29 years to go around the sun. In pictures he is depicted with a dark complexion and rides a chariot harnessed to a crow or vulture.

Legends say that when Shani first opened his eyes at birth, the sun went into eclipse, foreshadowing his influence on astrology. He was a great devotee of Krishna and spent his time immersed in thoughts about him. Marriage, however, changed Shani's life. Although Shani's wife was pious, she became jealous when she learned that her husband was more devoted to Krishna than to her. She tried to translate her romantic feelings for him into *maithuna*, but Shani ignored her and preferred meditation over *maithuna*. Enraged, she cursed him to be the carrier of evil eye. Thereafter Shani always looked downward, for his gaze had a destructive effect on anyone within his zone of vision.

The malefic effect of Shani's glance was on full display at the birth of Ganesha, the son of Shiva and Parvati. Like any proud mother, Parvati invited all the gods to their abode to celebrate the occasion. While the gods cooed and murmured at her beautiful baby, Shani stood at a distance, staring at the child's feet. Parvati felt sorry for Shani and invited

---

[50] The sun god Surya is described in detail in book 1 of this series.

Shani, the personification of the planet Saturn,
in a 19th-century painting by Raja Ravi Varma

him to look at the child. At first Shani tried to explain that nothing good ever came of his glance, but when Parvati insisted, Shani obeyed her and looked at the child. Instantly the child's head was burned to ash. Parvati fainted at the terrible tragedy. Meanwhile Shiva went looking for a replacement head to revive the child. The first creature he encountered was a bull elephant, so Shiva removed the elephant's head and surgically attached it to Ganesha's body.[51] Even with an elephant head, Ganesha looked beautiful, especially when he was in the company of elephants.

Meanwhile, at the heavens, Ravana became the undisputed king after defeating the gods in a battle. An astrologer himself, Ravana knew more than anyone how destiny was linked to the position of planets. He wanted to have the perfect planetary alignment during the birth of his first son. As time for the birth approached, Ravana arrested the rulers of planets. To keep their gazes away, he kept them under his feet with their heads facing downward. The gods were concerned that Ravana was gaming the planetary system to make his son invincible. They sent the sage Narada to Ravana's palace to sabotage this plan. When he observed the planetary lords lying flat on their stomachs, Narada asked Ravana to turn them over. Narada wanted Ravana to stomp their chests to mark his superiority over the gods. Ravana did not want to offend the sage, so he turned them over quickly, but even in that short moment, Shani's glance fell on Ravana.

Thereafter Ravana's life was never the same. Infuriated, Ravana locked Shani in a tiny cell with no windows so that no one could see his face. Hanuman later rescued Shani during his reconnaissance mission to Lanka. In fact Shani was so grateful to Hanuman that he promised his devotees would be immune to Shani's glance. Thus Hanuman became the succor for Shani's evil glance. For that reason he's known as Sankat Mochan, or the distress remover, and competes with Ganesha, the universal obstacle remover. For devotees, reading the verses of "Hanuman Chalisa" every day is supposed to alleviate the pain of Shani.

It is said that everyone goes through Sade Sati at least twice in their lifetime. Even gods are not exempted. When Shiva came under the influence of Shani, he experienced the loss of his wife, Sati, the first incarnation of Parvati. Hanuman did not get any exemption, even after

---

[51] This was another version of the story of how Ganesha lost his head. The original story is described in book 1 of this series.

rescuing Shani. Once, when Hanuman and Shani were together inside a cave, Shani climbed on Hanuman's shoulders to indicate that he was about to come under Shani's influence. Hanuman immediately assumed a larger size and crushed Shani's head on the ceiling. In pain, Shani begged Hanuman to release him and promised he would never torment him.

So is Sade Sati bad for everyone? Not everyone goes through a tough period when under the influence of Shani because it can vary considerably from person to person, depending on the planetary configuration of their birth chart. There are cases in history where people have even prospered under Shani's influence. Indira Gandhi, for instance, became the first woman prime minister of India when she was going through her Sade Sati. Even though Sade Sati is a difficult period for many, most people say that Sade Sati is also a period of great learning when valuable traits like patience, perseverance, endurance, and loyalty are forged into the character of a person.

Discerning readers will observe the glaringly inconsistent timelines in Shani's mythology. Shani is cursed, for instance, as the carrier of evil eye during or after Krishna's time, but Shani's malicious glance seems to be active even during the time of Rama. (Rama comes before Krishna in the Dashavataras.) Hindus explain this discrepancy by saying that Shani had cast his glance on Hindu chronology itself.

Most Hindu temples have a little shrine set aside for the Navagraha where Shani is placed along with the other planetary deities. Devotees usually appease these planetary gods before worshipping the main deity.

25

The Hundredth Monkey Phenomenon

> *The mind is like an iceberg,*
> *it floats with one-seventh of its bulk above water.*
>
> —SIGMUND FREUD, 1856–1939

In the 50s, scientists at the island of Koshima, Japan observed that when wild monkeys were fed with sweet potatoes, some took the potatoes to a nearby stream and washed them before eating. Monkeys love sweet potatoes, but not with dirt sticking on them. Soon more monkeys were found washing the potatoes. When the hundredth monkey in the island learned to wash potatoes, an amazing phenomenon happened. Colonies of monkeys on other islands and the mainland troop of monkeys in Takasakiyama started washing potatoes even though no physical contact existed between the potato-washing cult.

Did the addition of the hundredth monkey help reach the critical mass and raise the consciousness of monkeys on other islands? I don't know, but this question has vexed the scientific community without a definitive answer for many decades. The Indian philosopher-cum-speaker, Jiddu Krishnamurti, is often cited with the saying, "truth is a pathless land," meaning one can arrive at the truth in many ways.

By the way, is Hanuman or the Vanaras connected with this story? Nope. I tell you this monkey-related story to point out that, despite advances in science and technology, the mind is still a mystery. You think the mind is in your body? Or the body is in your mind? Hindus believe the mind and body are distinct. The body will perish, and so will the mind, but not all of it.

Based on its functions, the mind can be divided into the subconscious and the conscious. Science tells us that the subconscious mind coordinates the various functions of the physical body, such as adjusting hormone levels, controlling respiration and heartbeat, aiding digestion, and so forth. Unlike the subconscious mind, the conscious mind works directly with the brain and the five senses. When you learn a new skill, such as driving a car, you use your conscious mind. Having acquired the skill, you may drive to work without a conscious thought about how to drive. An activity that was conscious is now performed almost entirely by the subconscious mind. Awareness of oneself is also part of the conscious mind.

In Hinduism the subconscious mind is the storehouse of all *samskaras*—the imprints or experience of life, both past and present.[52] Furthermore, the sum total of your accumulated *samskaras* determines your personality, or who you are. Krishnamurti further states that our ancestral past often conditions the mind. The anchor of tradition, according to him, appears to be heavier in the East than in the West. For instance, unlike people in the West, Indians of all ages are predisposed to a religious mentality. While Krishnamurti underscored the influence of ancestral experience on individuality, the noted Swiss psychiatrist and psychoanalyst Carl Jung took this a step further. He postulated that the collective subconscious minds of people within a group form a shared

---

[52] Samskara also refers to the sacrament or rite that marks a significant transition of life, such as birth, marriage, or death.

network—or mind belt—in which they share elements of science, religion, and morality.[53]

So much for theory, but is it possible for consciousness to reach a critical mass? Not really, according to the author who conducted the study. After Dr. Lyall Watson first reported the hundredth monkey phenomenon, serious questions were raised about the authenticity of the study. Years later, Dr. Watson retracted from his original findings when he wrote, "It is a metaphor of my own making, based on very slim evidence and a great deal of hearsay. I have never pretended otherwise."

Despite Watson's frank admission, the notion of a critical mass of consciousness is so popular these days that several modern-day spiritualists promote it. Why does the story continue to gain traction even after the inventor of the story called it a metaphor? Maybe because this phenomenon is closely allied with the notion that every idea has a moment in time. When that time arrives, the idea springs into the minds of several people simultaneously. History abounds with stories of inventions made simultaneously in different regions of the globe.

Isaac Newton began his work on calculus in 1665. A few years later, when Gottfried Wilhelm Leibniz invented another form of calculus, critics accused him of stealing Newton's work, even though Leibniz was 650 miles away and living in a different country. Today both are credited with inventing calculus independently. The US inventor Thomas Edison is often credited with inventing the electric lightbulb, even though the British chemist Joseph Swan had demonstrated the first electric lightbulb much earlier. But Edison's bulb lasted longer and had a better design. The discovery of oxygen, the invention of the battery, the theory of evolution—all these scientific milestones were parented by more than one person at about the same time in different places.

The hundredth monkey phenomenon is often explained away by stating that we are part of each other and connected by the mind belt.

---

[53] Carl Jung used the term *unconscious*. For this discussion the terms *subconscious* and *unconscious* are interchangeable.

When the mind belt gradually accumulates enough voltage and exceeds a threshold, sparks are generated. At that moment—call it the critical mass or perfect storm of circumstances or crisis of consciousness—the same idea leaps into the minds of many people simultaneously, even if they are separated by vast distances. From this perspective, it's not surprising that Newton and Leibniz invented calculus separately at about the same time. The mind belt was buzzing with calculus, so calculus happened.

If you think the hundredth monkey phenomenon is bunkum, think again. If this phenomenon occurs with some regularity in regard to major scientific discoveries, what makes you certain it would not happen in other aspects of life?

> *There are two worlds: the world that we can measure with line and rule, and the world that we feel with our hearts and imagination.*
>
> —LEIGH HUNT, 1784–1859

26

Dashavataras and Darwin

The notion that science and spirituality are somehow mutually exclusive does a disservice to both.

— CARL SAGAN, 1934-1996

Spirituality and science are often viewed as bitter rivals, traveling on separate tracks on divergent roads. They may even appear as opposite pairs going by the principle of duality. Yet the domain of spirituality and science overlaps in more ways than we can fathom. These sworn enemies can sometimes be seen holding hands and sharing tales like the best of friends. One such moment of camaraderie occurs in cosmogony. Hindus, for instance, believe the life of our planet corresponds to a day of Brahma, or 4.32 billion years.[54] Modern science also claims, using radiometric dating, that the age of Earth is about 4.54 billion years. Another consensus between spirituality and science is found in the Hindu notion that the universe

---

[54] A day of Brahma is discussed in book 2 of this series.

is created, destroyed, and re-created in repetitive cycles. Contemporary physicists like Roger Penrose theorize that the Big Bang might be one in a cycle of such catastrophic events, suggesting that the universe has had multiple existences—thereby validating ancient Hindu beliefs.

Even more fascinating is the connection between modern evolution theory and the incarnations of Vishnu. Back in the 19th century, Charles Darwin first proposed that species arose from a single ancestor and became separated over time like branches of a tree. He hypothesized that aquatic creatures originated first, then amphibians, followed by land animals and airborne birds. Stunningly the sequence of incarnations in the ancient Hindu Dashavataras—from simple forms like fish and turtles at the beginning to more complex forms like *Homo sapiens* at the end—tracks evolution theory closely. Bizarre coincidence?

To be clear, Vishnu has more than ten avatars. In fact Pancharatra, a Vaishnava movement of the first millennium BCE, described 39 avatars of Vishnu. However, many Hindu sects singled out the top ten of Vishnu's incarnations—the Dashavataras—as representative of the rest. Even within the top-ten list we find variations, albeit minor ones. Although the notion of Dashavataras was known from ancient times, the 12th-century Sanskrit poet Jayadeva Goswami is credited with promoting this concept. As a result, the list compiled by Jayadeva became popular. After Darwin proposed his theory of evolution in 1859, many Hindu scholars—from both the East and West—noticed the striking correlation of evolution theory and Dashavataras. Prominent among them was the theosophist Helena Blavatsky, who suggested that Dashavataras were an allegorical presentation of Darwinian evolution. The Hindu social reformer Keshab Chandra Sen also saw Dashavataras as foreshadowing the modern theory of evolution. According to him, the Puranas had described evolution several centuries before Darwin, and evolution theory was a restatement of the Dashavataras. He also noted that many scholars were using this to point out that Hinduism is consistent with modern science.

Sen may have a point because Hindus do not accept evolution theory as it is commonly understood. Evolution theory says new species are

DASHAVATARAS AND DARWIN

The ten avatars of Vishnu. Counterclockwise from top left:
Fish, Turtle, Boar, Man-Lion, Dwarf, Parashurama, Rama, Krishna,
Buddha, and Kalki, depicted in a 19th-century painting by Raja Ravi Varma

created as a result of biological change, which is the slow process of adaptation to new environments over billions of years by living organisms. That is, species are created gradually over time based on their adaptation.[55] The Puranas, however, say all species are created simultaneously—not progressively. (For instance, human beings are part of the story of the Matsya avatar.) However, these species are at different levels of consciousness. Living beings are then placed in appropriate bodies according to their awareness level and evolve upward or downward according to their activities or mental disposition. In other words, the number of species is static, but the evolution or devolution of consciousness is dynamic. Bhaktivedanta Swami Prabhupada, the founder of the Hare Krishna movement, has this to say about evolution:

> *It is confirmed in Padma Purana that the species of life evolved from aquatics to plants, vegetables, trees; thereafter insects, reptiles, flies, birds, then beasts, and then humankind. This is the gradual process of evolution of species of life ... But we do not accept Darwin's theory. According to Darwin's theory, Homo sapiens came later on, but we see that the most intelligent personality, Brahma, is born first. So according to Vedic knowledge, Darwin or similar mental speculators are rejected so far as the facts are concerned.*

But Hinduism has always been an umbrella of traditions. Therefore not every Hindu sect accepts the avataric version of evolution. Detractors say Vishnu has innumerable avatars and to cherry-pick ten as his most representative is subjective and without basis. Furthermore, they point out that the Dashavataras is riddled with inconsistencies and anachronism. For instance, Bali, the generous king in the Vamana avatar (avatar #5) has a cameo in the Kurma avatar (avatar #2), even though Bali is the grandson of Prahlada (avatar #4). Additionally, the progression of consciousness, as suggested by avataric evolution, creates a dilemma. It implies Krishna is

---

[55] This also means humans could adapt and evolve into something else in the future.

superior to Rama in the level of consciousness because the Krishna avatar comes after the Rama avatar.

Yet it is indeed remarkable that the Puranas, compiled at least seven hundred years before Darwin, produced a list that more or less resembles modern evolution theory. The profundity of the Puranas was not lost on the British Sanskrit scholar Monier Monier-Williams, who wrote, "Indeed, the Hindus were Darwinians centuries before the birth of Darwin, and evolutionists centuries before the doctrine of evolution had been accepted by the Huxleys of our time." For the British scientist J. S. Haldane, the Dashavataras give a rough idea of vertebrate evolution: a fish, a tortoise, a boar, a man-lion, a dwarf, and then four men. The Indian philosopher Aurobindo Ghose regarded avataric evolution as a mythological narrative emphasizing the ascending scales of spiritual progress.

Religion is a culture of faith; science is a culture of doubt.
— RICHARD P. FEYNMAN, 1918–1988

Index

A

Adam's Bridge · **99-100**, 103
Aditi · 37-38
Agastya · 53, 66, 76
Agni · 14, 63, 78, 84, 105, 107-108
Agni Pariksha · 78, 84, **105-108**
ahimsa · 4
Airavata · 18-20
Amba · 47-50
Ambalika · 47-48
Ambika · 47-48
Amravati · 36
amrita · 16-19
Ananda Shesha · 13, 27
Angkor Wat · 20
Anjana · 120-121, 123
apsara · 120, 122
Archeological Survey of India · 103, 117
Arjuna · 12, 42, 46
Aryavarta · 5
ashrama · 82
Ashvamedha · 37, 79, 111
asura · 18, 33, 51
Aurangzeb · 117
avatar · 1, 3-5, 7-9, **11-15**, 19-21, 23, 25, 27-28, 32-35, 39-43, 45, 51, 55-56, 58, 60, 88, 92, 142, 144-145
Ayodhya · 58, 61, 63, 64, 66, 78-79, 107, 114-115, 117, 120, 122

Ayurveda · 90
Ayyappan · 20, 27, 121

B

Baber · 114-115, 117
Babri Masjid · **114-118**
Bāburnāma · 115
Badrinarayanan, S · 103
Balarama · 4, 13, 45, 56
Bali · 2-3, 18-19, **35-40**, 92-93, 144
Bhagavad Gita · 1, 7, 12
bhakti · 14, 84
Bharata · 13, 63-64, 66, 79, 120, 122
Bharucha · 114
Bhima · 123, 127
Bhishma · 47-50
Bhudevi · 22, 24-25
Bhuvarahaswami Temple · 25
Blavatsky, Helena · 142
boon of conditional immortality · 25, 36
Brahma · 1, 8-9, 14, 20, 22-23, 25, 29-30, 33, 35, 46, 58, 62, 71, 75, 79, 87, 91, 119, 127, 141, 144
Brahmastra · 76
Brahmin · 41-42, 44-45, 52-53, 88, 112
Brihaspati · 36
Britain · 99
British · 62, 99, 115, 139, 145

147

Buddha · 4-5, 13, 46, 56, 84, 101
Burdon, Eric · 14

C

Cameron, James · 11
Chandra · 17, 131
Chhaya · 132
chiranjeevi · 39, 46, 120
Chitrakuta Hills · 66
conscious mind · 138
Crystal, Billy · 93

D

Damayanti · 106
Dandaka · 64
Darwin, Charles · 141-145
Dashanana · 61, 91
Dasharatha · 62-66, 120
Dashavatara · **1-5**, 7, 13-14, 19, 21, 40, 45, 51, 53, 135, 141-142, 144-145
Delhi belly · 97
Densham, Pen · 81
deva · 19, 29, 35
Dhanavantari · 18
dharma · 3-4, 14, 28, 41, 44, 46, 49, 55, 78, 82-84, 91, 93, 107, 112
dharminator · 91
dhobi · 78, 107
Diti · 22, 28
Diwali · 58
Doordarshan · 113
Draupadi · 123

Durvasa · 15-17
Dussehra · 58, 87

E

Edison, Thomas · 139

F

Feltham, Owen · 15
Feynman, Richard P. · 145
Franklin, Benjamin · 112

G

Gandharva · 62, 91
Ganesha · 125, 132, 134
Ganges · 8
Garuda · 13
Gautama, Siddhartha · 4
Geological Survey of India · 103
Ghose, Aurobindo · 145
Goswami, Jayadeva · 142
Grogan, John · 34
Gyanavapi mosque · 117

H

Halahala · 17
Haldane, J.S. · 145
Hanuman · 58, 71-73, 75-76, 79, 92, 100, 103, **119-125**, 127, 129, **131-135**, 138

Hanuman Chalisa · 125, 134
Hastinapura · 48-49
Hayagriva · 8, 9
Hikayat Seri Rama · 58
Himalaya · 9, 43, 75-76, 120, 122
Hindu · 1, 3-5, 7, 11, 14-15, 19-20, 25, 27, 34-35, 39, 41, 44-46, 51, 53, 55-56, 58-59, 61, 82-83, 87, 89, 96, 101-102, 106, 110, 114-118, 127, 131, 135, 138, 141-145
Hindu Mahasabha · 116
Hinduism · 1, 4-5, 12, 19, 28, 33, 39, 46, 55-56, 61-62, 84, 87, 120, 138, 142, 144
Hiranya · 22, 29
Hiranyakashipu · 2, 22, 26, **28-33**, 35, 62, 91, 95
Hiranyaksha · **22-26**, 28, 62, 91
hundredth monkey phenomenon · **137-140**
Hunt, Leigh · 140

I

Ice Age · 25
incarnation (of Vishnu) · 1, 3-5, **11-12**, 38, 43, 45, 47, 63-64, 134
Indra · 14-16, 18-20, 22, 29-30, 35-39, 44, 75, 87, 121
Indrajit · 73, 75

J

Jagannath · 13
Jamadagni · 42, 44-45

Janaka · 64
Jatayu · 69-70, 129
Jaya · 21-22, 26, 28, 92
Jung, Carl · 138-139

K

Kaikesi · 88
Kaikeyi · 62-65
Kalanemi · 122
Kalaripayattu · 44, 53
Kalki · 4-5, 13
Kamadhenu · 44
Kamba · 57
Kambaramayana · 57
Kamsa · 4
Kanda
    Aranya · 61
    Ayodhya · 61
    Bala · 61, 111
    Kishkindha · 69
    Sundara · 69, 121, 125
    Uttara · 75, 107, 111
    Yuddha · 75
karma · 12, 29, 33, 109
Kartavirya Arjuna · 42, 44
Karya Siddhi Hanuman · 124
Kashyapa · 22, 28, 36-37
Kausalya · 62-63
Kaustubha · 17
Kennedy, John F. · 81
Kerala · 40, 46, **51-53**, 96-97, 101, 121
Kesari · 121
Ketu · 19
Khajuraho · 40

Khara · 67
Khordadbeh, Ibn · 100
Kishkindha · 69, 71
Kohli, Virat · 96
Konkan · 46, 52
Koshima · 137
Krishna · 1, 4-5, 9, 11-14, 19, 34, 45, 56, 81-82, 85, 122, 132, 135, 144-145
Krishnamurti, Jiddu · 138
Kshatriya · 41-45, 47, 49, 84, 88, 112
Kubera · 36, 61, 73, 91
Kumaras · 21, 25, 28, 92
Kumbhakarna · 26, 76, 92, 95
Kunti · 123
Kurma avatar · 2, 13, **15-21**, 107, 144
Kurukshetra War · 50
Kusha · 78-79, 111

L

Lakshmana · 58, 63, 65-67, 70-71, 75-76, 78-79, 84, 112, 120, 122
Lakshmana Rekha · 67
Lakshmi · 17, 58, 64
Lanka · 4, 56, 61-62, 68-69, **71-73**, 75, 78, 87, 90-93, 99-100, 101, 103, 107, 120, 122, 127, 129, 134
Lava · 78-79, 111
Laxman, V.V.S. · 96
Leibniz, Gottfried Wilhelm · 139-140
Lennon, John · 26
linga · 88
Luther King Jr, Martin · 118

M

Mahabali · 40, 51-53, 92-93, 120
Mahabharata · 4, 9, 12, 14, 44, 47, 50, 56, 85, 113, 122
Mahatma Gandhi · 27, 55, 60, 81, 97, 135
Mahendra Mountain · 46, 49
maithuna · 42, 121, 132
Malabar · 46, 52
Mandodari · 70, 92
Manthara · 62, 64, 66
Manu · 7-9
  Vaivasvata · 9
Manusmriti · 84
Marco Polo · 52
Maricha · 67
Maruti · 123
Maryada Purushottam · 55, 59, 82
Matsya avatar · 1, **7-9**, 13, 23, 40, 144
Maya Sita · 107-108
Meghanada · 75-76, 89
mind belt · 139-140
Mir Baqi · 115
Modi, Narendra · 114
Mohini · 18-20, 35, 121
moksha · 14
Monier-Williams, Monier · 145
Mount Kailash · 91
Mount Mandara · 17, 29
Mount Meru · 17, 73
Mughal · 114, 116
Mughal empire · 114
Muhammad of Ghazni · 117
Muslim · 53, 101-102, 114-117

N

Nair (community) · 53
Nala · 106
Nambudiri · 52
Narada · 29-30, 50, 73, 109, 134
Narasimha avatar · 2, 13, **27-34**, 39
National Remote Sensing Agency · 103
Navagraha · 131, 135
Neelakanta · 17
Nehru, Jawaharlal · 81, 116
Newton, Isaac · 139-140

O

Obama, Barack · 81, 97, 108, 125
Onam · 39, 53

P

Pancharatra · 13, 142
Pandava · 42, 123
Paramahamsa, Ramakrishna · 97
Parashurama · 3, 5, 13, **40-47**, 49, **51-53**, 56, 92, 120
Parashurama Devalaya · 46
Parashurama Kshetra · 52
Parashurameshwar Mandir · 46
Parijata · 17
Parvati · 17, 121, 132-134
pativrita · 59
Payovrata · 37
Pinaka · 45-46, 64
Pope John XXIII · 85
Prahlada · 30-33, 35-36, 144

pralaya · 7, 17, 20, 25
Praswapastra · 49
puja · 115-116
Purana · 9, 14, 34, 46, 52, 142, 144-145
  Agni · 14
  Bhagavata · 9, 14, 85
Pushpaka · 91
Putrakameshti · 63

R

Rahu · 19
Rahuketu · 18-19
rakshasa · 62-63, 66-67, 72-73, 76, 120
Rama · 3-5, 9, 11, 13-14, 19, 34, 40-43, 45-47, 51, **55-73**, 75-79, 81-85, 87-93, 100-103, 105, 107-120, 122-125, 127, 129, 135, 145
Rama Lalla · 115
Rama Lila · 58
Rama Navami · 58
Rama Setu · **99-103**, 120, 129
Ramakien · 58, 125
Ramanathaswamy Temple · 88
Ramancoil · 100
Ramaraj · 83
Ramayana · 3, 45, 56, 58-59, 61-62, 69, 75, 82, 84-85, 90, 100, 102-103, 105, **107-113**, 117, 121-122, 125, 127-128
  Kakawin · 58
  Valmiki · 56, 61, 107, **109-110**, 112
Rambha · 17
Ramcharitmanas · 57, 84

Rani Ki Vav · 40
Ratnakar · 109, 110
Ravana · 3-4, 26, 56, 58-59, 61-63, 66-73, 75-78, 82, 84, **87-93**, 99, 107-108, 119-120, 122, 127, 129, 134
Ravana Samhita · 89
Renuka · 42, 44
Rigveda · 14, 40
rishi · 8, 15

S

Sabarimala · 20
Sade Sati · **131-135**
Salva · 48, 49
Sampati · 129
samskara · 138
samudra manthan · 19
Sanjeevani · 75, 122
Sanjna · 132
Sankat Mochan · 131, 134
Sanskrit · 11, 22, 34, 58, 90, 110, 112, 125, 142, 145
Saptarishi · 109-110
Sarayu · 79
Saturn · 89, 131
Satyavan · 65
Satyavati · 48-49
Saugandhika · 123
Savitri · 65
Sen, Keshab · 142
Set Bandhai · 100
Shahi Idgah Mosque · 117
Shambuka · 83-84, 107, 112
Shani · 131-135
Shankhodara Temple · 9

Shantanu · 49
Sharanga · 17, 46
Shatapatha Brahmana · 9
Shatrughna · 63, 66, 79, 120
Shiva · 12, 17, 43-46, 52, 61-62, 64, 82, 88, 91-92, 101, 120-121, 132-134
Shiva Tandava · 91
Shudra · 83
Shukra · 36, 37, 38
Shurpanakha · 66-67, 84, 112
sindoor · 123
Singapore · 34
Singh (origin) · 34
Singh, Jyoti · 108
Sita · 45, 58, 64-65, 67-73, 78-79, 82, 84, 87, 91-92, **105-108**, 111-112, 123, 129
smriti · 110
Somnath Temple · 117
Sri Varahaswami Temple · 25
subconscious mind · 138-139
Sudarshana Chakra · 19
Sugriva · 71, 82, 103, 123, 128
Sumitra · 62-63
Surya · 7, 131-132
Sutala · 39
Swami Prabhupada · 97, 144
Swan, Joseph · 139
swayamvara · 45, 48, 64

T

Tadaka · 63
Takasakiyama · 137
tapas · 29, 62, 110

Tendulkar, Sachin · 96
Thampi, Sreekumaran · 27-28
Tolkien, J.R.R. · 34
Trikkakara Temple · 40
Trimurti · 29
Trivikrama · 14, 40
Tulsidas · 57, 84, 125
Tyagaraja · 119
Tzu, Lao · 10

U

Uchchaihsravas · 18-19
Ulagalantha Perumal Temple · 40
Uttararamacharita · 112

V

Vadakkunathan Temple · 46
Vaikuntha · 21, 25, 27, 28
Vaishnava · 10, 13, 142
Vaishrava · 88
Vali · 40, 71, 82, 84, 112
Valmiki · 56, 61, 69, 75, 78-79, 82, 84-85, 100, 107, **109-112**
Vamana avatar · 2, 13-14, 19, **35-40**, 51, 144
Vamana Temple · 40
Vanara · 100, 121, 123, **127-129**, 138
Varaha avatar · 2, 13, 21-25, 40
varna · 82
Varuni · 18
Vasco da Gama · 52
Vasuki · 17, 19
Vayu · 73, 120, 121, 123

Vayuputra · 123
Veda · 1-2, 8-9, 14, 36, 40, 59, 61, 83-84, 88, 91-92, 127
Vedanarayana Swami Temple · 9
veena · 88
Venkateswara · 13
Vibhishana · 73, 77
Vichitravirya · 48-49
Vijaya · 21-22, 26, 44, 46, 92
Vijaya bow · 44
Vindhya Mountain · 5, 66
Vishnu · 1-2, 4-5, 7-9, 11-14, 16-23, 25-40, 42-43, 45-47, 51, 56, 58, 62-63, 79, 85, 88, 91-93, 121-122, 142, 144
Vishvarupa · 7
Vishwajeet · 36
Vishwakarma · 39, 46, 73
Vishwamitra · 63-64
Vivekananda · 97-98

W

Wat Phra Kaew Temple · 58
Watson, Lyall · 139
Wheatley, Margaret J. · 41

Y

yajna · 36-37, 42, 63
Yama · 132
yuga
    Dvapara · 5, 45
    Kali · 4-5
    Treta · 5, 45, 51, 102

What's Coming Up?

Despite Vishnu having many avatars, the Dashavataras hold a special place in Hinduism today. We have described seven of the ten avatars in this book. Among them, the most-loved deity undoubtedly is Rama, the seventh incarnation. If you are searching for the perfect deity in the Hindu pantheon, look no further than Rama. Although Rama is especially revered among Hindus today, one deity beats Rama not only in popularity but also in the corpus of mythology.

Enter Krishna

Krishna is the single most beloved deity of the Hindu pantheon. He is often equated with Hinduism itself, and at times he is more revered than Vishnu, even though Krishna is only the eighth incarnation of Vishnu. (And, by the way, not everyone thinks Krishna is an incarnation of Vishnu.) Although Krishna is considered less morally perfect than Rama, he is more sociable and often celebrated for his artistic talents. We will look at Krishna in detail in book 4, starting with his extraordinary birth, followed by his childhood as a butter thief and later his amorous youth and dalliance with the *gopis* (cowherd girls). Later in life Krishna turns into a spiritual guru to his cousins in the great Mahabharata War. If the Ramayana presented some troubling moments for you, I am afraid the Mahabharata is full of them. The epic also introduces one of the great warriors of Hindu mythology—Arjuna. Although book 4 focuses on the Krishna avatar, we will also discuss the remaining avatars—thereby concluding the avatar saga.

www.ingramcontent.com/pod-product-compliance
Lightning Source LLC
Chambersburg PA
CBHW020652300426
44112CB00007B/352